Living with
Death

Living with Death

Osborn Segerberg, Jr.

26941

E. P. DUTTON & CO., INC.
New York

*The ornament used on each chapter opening
is an Oriental symbol for Longevity.*

Library of Congress Cataloging in Publication Data

Segerberg, Osborn, Jr.   Living with death

SUMMARY: Explores mankind's attitude toward death
throughout history, the implications of modern
technology on when and how we die, the acceptance of
death, the treatment of the dying and the dead, and the
way the living cope with death.

1. Death. [1. Death]   I. Title.
BD444.S43   128'.5   76-64   ISBN 0-525-33945-0

Published simultaneously in Canada by Clarke,
Irwin & Company Limited, Toronto and Vancouver

Designed by Meri Shardin
Printed in the U.S.A.
10 9 8 7 6 5 4 3 2

To Nan

Acknowledgments

I wish to thank Mrs. Janet Wedge for her interest and help, for allowing me to attend sessions of her death-education class at Yorktown High School, Yorktown Heights, N.Y., and for her detailed consideration of the manuscript. I wish to thank Richard Back, M.D., a surgeon of Kinderhook, N.Y., for reading the manuscript and for his suggestions concerning certain medical passages. I also wish to thank Lillian Kutscher of the Foundation of Thanatology for reading the manuscript and commenting on it. And I am indebted to Ann Troy at Dutton for her encouragement and careful editing of the manuscript.

Grateful acknowledgment is made for permission to quote from the following: *The Poems of Dylan Thomas,* copyright 1952 by Dylan Thomas, reprinted by permission of New Directions Publishing Corporation. An essay on death by Howard Hoyt, © 1971 by The New York Times Company, reprinted by permission. "A Loneliness I Never Expected," by Ralph Cokain, © 1972 by The New York Times Company, reprinted by permission. "A Rose for Emily" from *The Faulkner Reader* by William Faulkner, copyright © 1958 by Pantheon Books, a Division of Random Inc. *Doctor Zhivago* by Boris Pasternak, translated by Max Hayward and Manya Harari, revised by Bernard Guilbert Guerney, copyright © 1958 by Pantheon Books, a Division of Random

House, Inc., reprinted by permission. Speech by Emily, "I can't. I can't go on . . . every, every minute?" on page 100 of *Our Town* by Thornton Wilder, copyright 1938, © 1957 by Thornton Wilder, reprinted by permission of Harper & Row, Publishers, Inc.

Contents

 ONE

The Discovery
of Certain Death

Olivia was alone now in the house and suddenly the lights went out. She shuddered, then tried the light switch on the wall beside her. It clicked, but there was no light. She must hold down the panic bubbling up within her. Why had she ever come here? Olivia had but one thought, one objective. Get out of this house. Feeling along the wall, she slowly began to descend the creaking stairs, step after cautious step. She thought she heard a noise. She stopped and held her breath. She could hear nothing over the pounding of her heart. At the bottom of the stairs she suddenly felt two cold hands closing around her neck. A scream froze in her throat. . . .

Who hasn't looked up from a mystery story late at night to re-assure oneself of safe surroundings? Then back one goes, turning page after page to find out what happens. Why? Who done—or as purists insist—did it?

We learn all the answers at the end, of course. Sherlock Holmes or the detective from the local precinct solves the mystery. We can go to sleep safe and snug, thankful for the more commonplace events of our own lives.

The fact is, though, that these mysteries are merely little puzzles compared to the granddaddy of them all, the Mystery of Death. You are a participant in that one.

1

The fact of death is obvious enough, and common enough, too. It is reported on television news or in a newspaper—if not on the front page, then certainly on the obituary page. It usually doesn't bother us much, although the account of a murder nearby stirs anxiety.

Initiation into the mystery begins with the death of someone important to us. A precious person who has been present always is lost forever; a living entity one moment is nonliving the next. Life, the essence of that being, disappears. And lost with it is all further chance for happiness, all further chance to see the world's beauty, all further chance to realize his or her potential to do good things in this life. We can never talk to this person again. Thinking about such an event under the pressure of intense emotions forces to the surface a piece of knowledge we usually keep locked up and hidden within us: I, too, will die! I, too, have only a limited time to experience life. And then. . . .

Now, this mystery has been considered, studied, worried over not by a few fictional sleuths but by armies of investigators: by every human being who has lived. Not that everyone has sought new or original solutions, but everyone must have answers to such questions as: Why? Why me? How does death come about?

Here is one answer. Once upon a time an old woman lived in a village with her daughter and granddaughter. One day the grandmother and granddaughter went to bathe in the stream that ran beside their village. The girl remained on shore while the grandmother went far into the creek until she was out of the girl's sight. Then the old woman shed her old, wrinkled skin and let it float away. This changed her into a young girl, and with this new appearance she returned to the shore. The granddaughter, not recognizing her grandmother, was afraid. She would not permit the apparent stranger to come ashore and instead ordered her away. The grandmother was humiliated and angry. She went back into the creek and searched for her old skin. She finally found it caught upon a bush. She put it on once again and returned to her granddaughter, who recognized her this time and welcomed her. "A young girl came here," the granddaughter said. "I was afraid and I chased her away." They went home, and the grandmother told her daughter: "I went to bathe and the current carried my skin away. Your daughter did not recognize me and ordered me away. I shall not slough my skin again. We shall all become old. We shall die."

That myth is told and believed by Trobriand islanders in the Southwest Pacific. On the other side of the world, in Africa, the Galla people say that God sent the bird Holawaka to tell human beings that when they found themselves growing old and weak, they should slip off their skins and they would become young again. On the way, the bird came upon a serpent eating a dead animal. Holawaka asked to share the food. The snake agreed but only on condition that the bird reveal God's message. This is the reason why snakes can shed their skins and grow young again while human beings must die.

Before hooting at these "explanations" of why we grow old and die, consider that the desire for eternal youth burns as brightly today as at any time in the past. People spend billions of dollars on cosmetics, health clinics, youthful clothes with one objective: to stay young or, at least, *look* young. Some wealthy, aging adults go to expensive clinics to have their faces "peeled." They have the outer layer of skin peeled away. There is great danger of infection in this procedure. The patients must remain secluded in highly sterilized quarters. They wouldn't want to be seen by other people anyway, because their faces look like skinned tomatoes. Their reward for this ordeal is that when the new layer of epidermis grows back, it has the smooth appearance of youth. The person looks young again, like the grandmother in the myth. This transformation is only skin-deep, alas, and after awhile the telltale wrinkles reappear. The person must shed his skin again or become resigned to looking his age.

It was the *appearance* of rejuvenation after a snake had shed its skin that led our primitive ancestors to conclude that the serpent could renew its youth and avoid death—that it possessed the secret of living eternally. Primitives often enough confused appearance with reality. This is understandable, for we still can be deceived by appearances. But when *we* find ourselves in error, we are far more likely to look for the fault in our reasoning.

Primitives, on the other hand, believed they knew the secret of how nature worked and, possessing this power, could command nature's obedience. The method of thinking by which early human beings believed they could produce the effects they wanted is known to us today as magic. Imitative magic was based on the principle that like produces like. For instance, when a Hottentot priest in South Africa causes a fire to send up billows of cloud-like smoke in order to bring rain, he is practicing imitative magic. Some primitive human beings copulated in the fields at the time of spring planting in order to encourage the fertility of the land by their example.

Contagious magic was based on the belief that things which come into contact exert an effect on each other and can continue to do so at a distance. The most common example of this mistaken association of ideas in the primitive world was the belief that parts of a person, such as hair or nail clippings, exerted an influence upon him even after they were severed. Therefore, if a person could get possession of a piece of his enemy's clothing or some of his hair, he would have the means of harming his adversary. Cannibalism was practiced in the belief that by eating the human being, one took over his strength and virtue.

Even the accidental coming-together of words or thoughts with some desired event could give them the contagious magic of contact. A ritual or incantation that happened to precede the event became indelibly associated with the effect. And, according to the reasoning of magic, repetition of the word formula would, presto, produce the effect again. We see this kind of thinking in operation today when a football coach, say, happens to be wearing a certain hat when his team wins an important game and ever after wears his "lucky" hat on game days, hoping it will produce the desired effect—victory.

If this is a hit-and-miss form of reasoning, one kind of magic worked with eerie regularity. Voodoo death. Many primitives believed that by making some article stand for the person of an enemy and then by inflicting damage to the substitute (a form of imitative magic), one could injure or kill the person. Simply pointing a bone at the victim or pronouncing a curse upon him would suffice. A famous medical researcher, Walter Cannon, cited this case at a sugar plantation in Queensland, Australia:

> One day a Kanaka came to his [Dr. P. S. Clarke's] hospital and told him he would die in a few days because a spell had been put upon him and nothing could be done to counteract it. The man had been known by Dr. Clarke for some time. He was given a very thorough examination, including an examination of the stool and urine. All was found normal, but as he lay in bed he gradually grew weaker. Dr. Clarke called upon the foreman of the Kanakas to come to the hospital to give the man assurance, but on reaching the foot of the bed, the foreman leaned over, looked at the patient, and then turned to Dr. Clarke, saying, "Yes, doctor, close up him he die" [that is, he is nearly dead]. The next day, at 11 o'clock in the morning, he ceased to live. A postmortem examination revealed nothing that could in any way account for the fatal outcome.

Now, while this death appeared mysterious to the scientist, it seemed obvious enough to the primitive. He knew that poisons, wounds, falls, burns are natural causes of death, but "natural" for the other fellow. The closer death came to him, the more likely he was to believe that it had a magical cause instead of a natural one. He believed he was the victim of some other person's evil intent—some person alive or dead, because the primitive's world was populated with both kinds of beings.

By applying the rule of similarity that is the basis of imitative magic, we can see how early human beings concluded that there is existence after death. Living close to nature, they were witnesses to the great seasonal demonstrations of death and rebirth. Surely if nature practiced resurrection on such a grand scale, it must apply as well in the case of human death.

In studies in many parts of the world earlier in this century, Sir James Frazer and other anthropologists learned that primitive people almost universally believed that a person's spirit or soul continued to exist after physical death. According to the primitive system of belief known as animism, all living things had souls, and some nonliving objects as well. Motions, shadows, reflections, echoes were easily mistaken for living things. The first human beings could not be sure that the roiling thunderhead, giving off roars and lightning bolts and often assuming shapes that resembled living forms, was inanimate. From there, it does not take much more imagination to believe in the resident god, the cloud's soul or anima.

Belief in the spirit world shaped primitive medicine and led to the first surgery. In many excavations, archaeologists discovered Stone Age skulls with holes about the size of a nickel or quarter. The scientists knew that the holes had not been the cause of death because of evidence that the bone had grown in an attempt to heal. Some skulls had several of these holes, one as many as five. The holes were a puzzle. What did they mean?

It is now agreed that the holes were cut into the skulls by witch doctors treating victims of epilepsy. With that brain ailment the sufferer thrashes around in an uncontrollable fit. Primitive people reasoned that the sick person was inhabited or possessed by a demon. The remedy for that was to make it possible for the evil spirit to get out by performing the first surgery, cutting holes in the skull.

If the demon refused to leave, the witch doctor resorted to exorcism. He tried to drive the devil out with incantations, prayers, fasting. He tried frightening the demon with loud noises and wild posturings, threatening gestures. He tried beating the person.

Almost everywhere, primitive men and women regarded the spirits of the dead with one common emotion: fear. They knew how cantankerous a person can be when alive and meant to take no chances with spirits. Careful not to give offense, they thoughtfully provided food and other necessities and observed all the courtesies that the person's rank demanded. They even held annual feast days for the departed spirits. There were enough problems with the living without risking trouble from the dead.

Underlying these attitudes was the fear of death itself, dread of the corpse, sorrow for the lost person. Despite the primitive's confidence in a survival beyond death, he was reluctant to approach this fate. In speaking with several seriously ill South Sea islanders, anthropologist Bronislaw Malinowski wrote: "I felt, half-expressed and roughly formulated, but still unmistakable in them all, the same melancholy sorrow at the transience of life and all its good things, the same dread of the inevitable end, and the same questioning as to whether it could be staved off indefinitely or at least postponed for some little time. "

And this is where myths come in. Myths helped to make the whole painful subject more manageable. They helped our ancestors to deal with an unbearable reality that was discovered by their sharpened intelligence. The myth about the grandmother reduces the apprehension over death to a trivial domestic spat. The longed-for power to achieve eternal youth is lost by a small accident that could have been prevented by an old woman and young girl. In the message that failed, the Holawaka myth, the issue is taken completely out of human hands. In another common African myth on the origin of death, God gives humankind a choice. God holds the nucleus of death in one hand and the nucleus of immortality in the other. A human being picks the wrong hand. Sometimes you win, sometimes you lose: the theory of probabilities long ago.

From his studies of comparative mythology, anthropologist Frazer believed that the story of Adam and Eve and the forbidden fruit was an attempt to explain human mortality: to account for how death originated. At first, Frazer maintained, the two trees in the Garden of Eden were the tree of life and the tree of death. God told Adam and Eve to eat the fruit of the tree of life and to avoid the tree of death. However, the serpent deceived them into choosing the wrong tree and gained for itself the power of rejuvenation by shedding its skin.

Some time later, Frazer believed, the tree of death in the myth was changed to the tree of the knowledge of good and evil. If we accept Frazer's interpretation, what, then, was this knowledge that by itself could create the first human beings? For that transformation was brought about by Adam and Eve's eating fruit from the tree of the knowledge of good and evil.

The conventional answer was that the first man and woman were awakened to their sexual differences. They suddenly realized they were naked and so covered themselves. But this has never been a satisfactory explanation, particularly if you believe that sex is a natural and not an evil part of life. Besides, the knowledge of the difference between the sexes is hardly unique with human beings.

In order to find the solution to those questions we must ask: What makes us different from other creatures? There's not much trouble deciding when we compare ourselves with a frog or a butterfly. Although even here we must remember that all members of the animal kingdom are composed of the same basic materials: nucleic acids and sub-protein amino acids. This is one reason why scientists believe that life on earth had one beginning and then evolved to its present diversity.

When we limit considerations to mammals, our distinctiveness is further diminished. All mammals maintain constant internal temperatures, conceive and nurture offspring within the mother, then provide care for the young. Many mammal species are social animals. When we come to the primates, similarities abound. Chimpanzees have been observed using sticks as tools to get at termites for food. And in the last few years we have seen that chimps can be taught words and even sentences. They are capable of symbolic thinking.

With all that, we are the only animal that ever walked upright continually on two legs. This position freed the hands from loco-motion. Our hominid ancestors of more than 2 million years ago were able not only to *use* tools but to *make* them. Tool-making requires a different kind of thought process: the capacity to en-visage an imaginary future situation. This pioneering venture of thinking in abstract concepts led to the development of speech, language, mathematics—and all the accomplishments of modern civilization.

It led also to a bleak and haunting discovery. We die. Inevitably.

The origin-of-death myths are a prehistoric intellectual record of the human effort to grapple with this fearsome mystery. Through archaeological finds that can be dated, we are learning how very long the effort has been going on. In the Shanidar cave in northern Iraq, scientists came upon a Neanderthal hunter's grave estimated to be sixty thousand years old. A study of the soil around the grave revealed an extraordinary amount of pollen. The pollen indicated that the body had been laid to rest with masses of flowers, bright-colored blossoms related to grape hya-cinth, bachelor's button, and hollyhock. Some of the plants found by the grave are still used by people in Iraq as herbal remedies. Perhaps the plants were placed with the dead hunter in the hope that their medicinal value would help him in his afterlife. Perhaps the Neanderthal survivors offered the flowers from the same emo-tions of reverence, sorrow, and love that motivate us at funerals today.

Searchers have found many prehistoric human graves from

Neanderthal down through Neolithic times (Neanderthal man emerged in Europe somewhere around a hundred thousand years ago, the New Stone Age lasted from about 9000 B.C. to about 5000 B.C.). The dead person was buried with care. Interred with the body were carved tools and, the presence of animal bones indicates, food—provisions for the dead person's spirit on its journey beyond death. These bequests from the living to the dead indicate an entirely new appreciation of life and death.

The grave is the artifact, the handiwork, of a new kind of creature, the first and only one to bury its dead. Many animals appear distraught when one of their group dies. Elephants have been observed trying to revive a dying member of the herd, even attempting to lift it to its feet with their tusks. Anthropologist Jane Goodall observed a young chimpanzee that grieved to death after its mother died. All animals can distinguish between a living organism and a carcass. Mimicking death, or "playing possum," is a defensive technique of many species.

But no other nonhuman creature lives its lifetime with the knowledge of its own certain death.

An interpretation of the Adam and Eve myth made here from the previous statement is that the fruit of the tree of the knowledge of good and evil opens one's eyes to the certainty of death. That is the knowledge of evil. With that discovery comes realization of how good life is, how precious—precisely because it *is* limited. It does not go on forever. One cannot live happily ever after. Knowledge of good and evil—of fleeting life and inevitable death—means exile from the Garden of Eden, the paradise of blessed innocence that shields other living things from their fate. That knowledge created the first human beings.

A final heroic attempt to return to this paradise is told in the Babylonian epic of Gilgamesh. This story was discovered recorded on clay tablets, and it goes back into the more ancient Sumerian civilization.

Gilgamesh, the child of a goddess and a mortal father, is king of Uruk, one of the Sumerian cities that flourished along the Euphrates River from about 3800 B.C. to 2000 B.C. During his reign, Gilgamesh becomes a despot, ravishing maidens and forcing young men to work excessive hours on the city's defense walls. The people pray to the gods for relief from this oppression and the gods respond by creating Enkidu, a wild-looking man with tremendous strength.

Enkidu comes into Uruk and challenges Gilgamesh. A titanic struggle takes place in the city square. Gilgamesh and Enkidu fight like infuriated bulls until Gilgamesh finally subdues his rival. After that, they become great friends.

With his new companion, Gilgamesh sets off in search of adventure and everlasting fame. They slay an ogre in the sacred cedar forest and later kill a divine bull sent against Uruk by the goddess of love because Gilgamesh spurned her proposal of marriage. Gilgamesh exults in the victorious salvation of the city, and his people hail him as "the most glorious among heroes."

Enkidu, however, not content with the slaying of the bull, insults the goddess. That night he dreams of a meeting of the gods and their decision to punish one of the two heroes for their arrogant acts. The lot falls to Enkidu. He becomes ill and dies.

Gilgamesh is overcome with grief. He refuses to give Enkidu's body up for burial, hoping somehow that his lamentations will revive his friend. But after seven days and nights, Gilgamesh admits that the attempt is hopeless. Enkidu is buried with honors.

Gilgamesh leaves Uruk and roams in the desert, inconsolable. But this time he is wracked by fear of his own death. "When I die," he asks, "shall I not be like unto Enkidu?"

Gilgamesh can conquer his despair only by aspiring to escape the fate of humankind. He sets out to see Utnapishtim (the

Babylonian equivalent of Noah), who was rewarded with immortality for saving humanity from destruction in the great flood. Gilgamesh crosses several mountain ranges and finally arrives at a sea. He goes to the divine barmaid, Siduri, to explain his mission and find out how he can cross the sea to visit Utnapishtim. Siduri advises him to go home and accept his fate. She explains to him that there is no escape from death. But Gilgamesh persists, and finally she discloses that Utnapishtim's boatman is on their shore. Gilgamesh leaves the goddess and persuades the boatman to take him to his master.

Immortal Utnapishtim tells his visitor that he was rewarded with eternal life for performing a superhuman service to humanity. What can Gilgamesh do to earn such a prize? There seems to be no answer. But after some thought Utnapishtim proposes that Gilgamesh stay awake for six days and seven nights. If he can overcome sleep, perhaps he can master death as well.

The hero, however, is exhausted from his journey and soon falls asleep.

Having failed, a dejected Gilgamesh starts back in the boat. But as he is leaving, Utnapishtim tells him of a wondrous plant that can rejuvenate a person when he grows old. The problem is that the plant is at the bottom of the sea. This time Gilgamesh is determined not to fail. He descends to the sea's depths and with a superhuman effort retrieves the plant. Now, with unbounded joy, he starts back for Uruk. On the way he stops by a clear pool for a delicious swim, and in his absence a snake eats the plant, thus gaining for itself the power to shed its skin and renew its life. Gilgamesh weeps bitterly when he finds that he has lost this final chance to escape death.

But since there is nothing he can do about it, he decides to return to Uruk and be content with his lot. He is ready to heed the advice of Siduri to take pleasure from his work and, in the great city he built, to live joyfully with his wife and their children.

This story was told over and over in the early civilizations of the Middle East. Its lesson is clear. If even a Gilgamesh cannot escape from death, then all mortals must learn to come to terms with their destiny.

 TWO

The Evolving Look
of Death

Shanti Devi was born in Delhi, India, in 1926. At the age of three, she began remembering details of a former life. Her name had been Lugdi, Shanti told her parents, and she lived in Mathura, a city about eighty miles away. During the next few years, Shanti filled in details of this former life. She had been born in 1902, married a cloth merchant named Kedar Chaubey, given birth to a son, and then died ten days later. By the time Shanti was nine years old, her family had begun checking her story. They wrote to Chaubey. His reply confirmed her story. Chaubey sent a relative to visit the Devi home and later came himself unannounced. Each time, Shanti recognized the visitors.

On Shanti's first visit to Mathura, she identified Chaubey's house and accurately described its layout, including closets. She was taken to Lugdi's parents' home and picked them out of a crowd of more than fifty people. At a third dwelling, one belonging to Chaubey's family, Shanti said she—or rather Lugdi—had buried money in the corner of a particular room. Searchers began to dig and found nothing. They dug deeper and came upon a place where valuables had been kept. It was empty.

At that point, Chaubey admitted that he had taken the money after his wife's death.

Many, many such reincarnations are reported in India, but the

14

case of Shanti Devi was studied and authenticated by independent investigators. "The accounts available to me indicate that Shanti Devi made at least twenty-four statements of her memories which matched the verified facts," says Ian Stevenson, a parapsychologist, or scientific investigator of psychic phenomena, who specializes in studying reincarnations. "No instances of incorrect statements are recorded."

Dr. Stevenson's investigations revealed to him that Chaubey often traveled from his native city of Mathura to Delhi to buy cloth. While in Delhi, Chaubey would go to a candy shop that was within yards of the Devi home. Shanti saw him there one day as she was passing by on her way home from school. This would be years after her first reports of a former life, but the coincidence opens the possibility that she could have seen him years earlier. "I have the impression that the more one penetrates into these cases the more one is likely eventually to find some person or persons who have known both families or, failing that, known both areas," says Dr. Stevenson. He conjectures, since hoax or collusion has been ruled out in too many instances, that the information may somehow be transmitted through telepathy and extrasensory perception.

Dr. Stevenson finds that most reported reincarnations begin with small children, usually two to four years old. He also finds that most occurrences take place where people *believe* in reincarnation. The memories of American children are not so rich, he says. Some of us may have experienced the uncanny feeling of déjà vu—already knowing a situation upon first encounter—or of thinking of someone and then receiving a telephone call from that person. But we tend not to dwell on such events for long.

In the West, reported survival after death takes a different form. This is a case cited in the *Journal of the American Society for Psychical Research:*

A man named William Smith was senior warden, treasurer,

and chief contributor of a small Episcopal church in New England. Smith discovered that financial investments he had made with church funds had suffered sharp losses. He felt guilty and depressed as well over the transactions. He could not make up the losses to the church because his own fortunes had suffered in the same venture.

On Easter morning, he was at his accustomed place in church and passed the collection plate as usual, but his friends noted that he appeared despondent. He committed suicide the next day.

The following Sunday, another man substituted for Smith and took up the collection with the second warden. After the two men had passed the plates, they returned to the chancel steps. As they stood there, the rector, who was waiting to receive them, was seen to stagger backwards as though stunned. His cousin, a Miss Barry who was in a front pew to the left of the aisle, was startled by her cousin's appearance. At that moment, she observed that there were three men standing at the chancel steps, and the third man was William Smith. The next instant, she heard a woman shriek from the other side of the church.

As soon as the service ended, Miss Barry asked her cousin what had happened. He hesitated, then said, "I thought I saw. . . ."

"I know what you saw," she interrupted. "I saw him, too. William Smith was in church this morning in his accustomed place."

"Yes," the rector answered.

A few days later, another woman confirmed that she had screamed because she saw Smith standing at the chancel steps. Each of the three witnesses perceived Smith from a different angle, although no one else in the church detected the apparition.

A ghost or a triple hallucination?

Ghosts are the tradition in the West. People in most early civilizations believed that the person's shade persisted after death, inhabiting some underworld place. When Odysseus goes to Hades, he must revive the enfeebled replicas of once-living beings with a drink of sheep's blood. These phantoms resemble but are pale shadows of their former living selves. Cicero says it was generally believed that the dead lived beneath the earth, and every Roman town had a trench that was regarded as the entrance to the lower world. The trench was vaulted over with a hole left in the vault to be closed by a stone of the dead. Corn was thrown into the trench, which was filled with earth, and an altar erected over it. On three solemn days of the year—August 25, October 5, and November 8—the stone was removed so that the spirits of the dead could return and be honored.

The Greeks and Romans placed immense importance upon burying a dead person, making a necessity of that human custom begun in the haze of prehistory. These ancients believed that the spirits of the unburied were not at rest, but trapped between the worlds of the living and the dead. Their specters roamed about and could communicate with the living, even haunt them. These ghosts were not subject to the regulations of the state. Neither were the spirits of those persons who died violent deaths, who were murdered, who were executed for crimes, who died before their time. These spirits not at rest were evil.

Socrates, the champion of rationality who ridiculed the gods of Mount Olympus, believed in ghosts. These wicked souls have become so attached to their physical bodies, he said, that they are afraid to leave and so they hover about graveyards. Plato has Socrates say in the *Phaedo*: "They continue wandering until at last, through craving for the corporeal, which unceasingly pursues them, they are imprisoned once more in a body. And as you might expect, they are attached to the same sort of character or nature which they have developed during life."

The unquestioning acceptance of ghosts persisted for two thousand years after Socrates. Shakespeare in the seventeenth century wrote into the plays *Macbeth* and *Hamlet* for his believing audiences the ghosts of Banquo and Hamlet's father—both murdered men. Samuel Johnson, a razor-sharp intellectual of eighteenth-century London, said he believed in ghosts because all races of men everywhere in all ages had reported apparitions of the dead. But the rise of science, with its proof, proof, proof, forced specters, phantoms, phantasms to retreat to fictional ghost stories. To most people, real live ghosts became—well, unbelievable.

Halloween is a vestige of that ancient ceremony when spirits of the dead were officially allowed out to be honored. But the only ghosts, goblins, and skeletons we see today are children's costumes.

It is one of those quirks of history that Houdini, a master magician and possibly the greatest escape artist of all time, died on Halloween, 1926. Houdini had been buried countless times before his death. Of his many "challenges of death," one was to be sealed into a coffin, the coffin then lowered six feet into the ground, and the "grave" filled with earth. He remained there while assistants and spectators waited anxiously for one hour. At the appointed time, assistants shoveled away the dirt, the coffin was raised and opened, and Houdini sat up and smiled.

The difficulty of this feat can be gauged by imagining yourself confined inside that coffin with six feet of earth on top of you. If you called for help, no one would hear you, and even if people could hear, they would never be able to reach you in time if there were a real emergency. "My chief task has been to conquer fear," Houdini once said. "[W]hen I am buried alive under six feet of earth, it is necessary to preserve absolute serenity of spirit. If I grow panicky I am lost."

Houdini's powers were so impressive that Sir Arthur Conan Doyle, the creator of Sherlock Holmes, was convinced that they were psychic powers. It is ironic that the author of the detective who always triumphed through logic and deduction was himself a devout believer in spiritualism. Doyle believed Houdini was a true medium who was crassly using his occult abilities to amuse people and make a fortune.

As it happened, Houdini knew about mediums, seances, and "communicating" with the dead. In order to get out of circus work, he had turned to that form of spiritualism with his wife earlier in his career. She learned how to "fall into a trance," while "Professor" Houdini picked up odd bits of information by visiting grave sites and noting tombstones, visiting homes as a survey-taker, attending places where he could eavesdrop on local gossip, and by employing tipsters. These bits of personal information were divulged by the medium, of course, during the seance. Both Houdinis were so clever at this line of work that they were establishing a reputation, but at the same time they felt uneasy about hoodwinking people with fake "messages." When a "prophecy"—no more than a guess by Houdini—came true, he decided to get out of the medium business.

Still. . . . After the death of his mother, to whom he was extraordinarily devoted, he wondered if there might just possibly be a spark of truth where so many were willing to believe. He tried to communicate with his mother, and after each failure he would stand beside her grave and announce: "I have heard nothing yet."

Sir Arthur's wife, Lady Doyle, claimed to be a medium, and one day the Doyles and Houdini gathered for a private seance. At this sitting, Houdini wanted to believe, tried to believe. Lady Doyle went into a trance and began writing on a pad what was purported to be a message to Houdini from his mother. But Houdini's steel-trap mind could not accept the generalities handed to him as genuine. In life, his mother spoke almost entirely in Yiddish. The message was in English. The day happened to be her birthday. There was no mention of it. Neither did the message refer to him in any of the intimate terms his mother used.

Perhaps because of profound disappointment at this effort, Houdini began a one-man crusade of exposing mediums as frauds. No one was better equipped for the job. Singlehandedly, he virtually laid to rest one of the last forms of the ancient human belief that the ghosts of the dead can interact with the living.

But Houdini could never allay his own suspicion that there

might be some hidden truth behind spiritualism. He made elaborate arrangements to get in touch with his wife after he died. If anyone could penetrate the barrier, he felt, he could. After Houdini's death, his widow followed his instructions, went to the appointed locations, but there was no communication from the great magician. We should not be surprised. Houdini, after all, was not a master of science but of magic—the primitive method of thinking that had difficulty separating truth from appearance and finally turned into the skilled presentation of illusion.

Through recorded history, the human response to death spread across a full spectrum of attitudes, most of them elaborations and refinements of the original ones. "Whatsoever thy hand findeth to do, do it with thy might; for there is no work, nor device, nor knowledge, nor wisdom, in the grave, whither thou goest," advised the Book of Ecclesiastes in the Bible. The language and philosophy of this book are similar to the epic of Gilgamesh. Live happily with the person you love, enjoy your work, "eat thy bread with joy, and drink thy wine with a merry heart . . . for that is thy portion in this life."

In time, this wisdom could be corrupted into the hedonistic "Eat, drink, and be merry, for tomorrow we die"—a cynical recommendation to forsake any meaningful existence. Or it could sour into the pessimism expressed by Sophocles when he wrote that never to have been born is best and to die quickly second best. The English poet Lord Byron offered the bittersweet "Whom the gods love, die young."

Epicureanism, one of the important philosophies of the Greek and Roman world, held that we are made of atoms and therefore death means dissolution—annihilation. Existentialists today have carried this reasoning to its extreme. Not only is death extinction, but every future moment of your life is not to be counted on. You may be killed by an automobile two minutes from now or a meteorite in the next instant may destroy your city. Therefore, the only thing to do, the existentialists say, is to live each moment to the fullest extent, getting as much as possible from the time you are sure you do have.

At the other extreme, Plato conceived of an independent soul, one that pre-existed before joining the body and went on eternally after separation at death. Most religions, however, conceived of a soul that began with the person and an afterlife based on rebirth or resurrection.

The Hindu belief in reincarnation and transmigration of souls meant that a person's being lived on indefinitely, rekindled after death in another human body or some other form. Reincarnation at first was a joyful celebration of life. But around 1500 B.C. white-skinned Aryans invaded India and enslaved many of the dark-skinned inhabitants. In order to reinforce their domination, the conquerors developed the caste system. In this organization that was both religious and social, the priests, or Brahmans, were considered the head; warriors the arms; bankers, tradesmen, and gentleman farmers the trunk; and servants and laborers—most of the dark-skinned native people—the feet, at the bottom of society. *Karma* was the instrument to enforce the caste system, rewarding caste virtues and punishing sins against the system. If members of the lowest orders performed their menial jobs meticulously well, they could hope for promotion to a higher caste, but it might take hundreds or even thousands of reincarnations. On the other hand, derelictions of duty were punishable by demotions down the ladder to vermin and insects. It is for this reason that members of the Jain sect will kill no living animal and the Jain monk carries a broom to sweep insects from his path.

The misery of low-caste life united with the belief that a person was fated to a series of repetitions gradually transformed the concept of perpetual rebirth into a life-hating concept. It meant perpetual imprisonment with no relief. Suicide was not a way out, because one merely reappeared in a similar or worse situation. One must break the cumulative cause-and-effect wheel of karma and rebirth.

It was to these downtrodden people and this unjust condition that Buddha appeared as a savior. The way to break the law of karma and the cycle of rebirth, Buddha taught, is to attain peace of mind through controlling worldly desires. Not merely sensual desires, but desire for wealth, power, fame, beauty, advantage, success. It is possible, he said, through right actions and thoughts, through self-purification and the pursuit of saintliness, to achieve a state of perfect serenity. This is nirvana. While Buddha never said so explicitly, what he was offering tormented souls in effect was the peace of—death.

In the same sixth century B.C. in which Buddha was born in India, Zoroaster in Persia was preaching a religion of resurrection. The world was locked in a titanic struggle, Zoroaster taught, between a God of light and good and a prince of darkness and evil. At stake in the contest was each human soul, for with free will each person had to make his own choice between good and evil. The final phase of the conflict began with the appearance of Zoroaster. The fight would be carried forward by three descendants to be born in later ages. The last one would be the Sayoshant, or savior. At the end, the forces of good would defeat the forces of evil in an apocalyptic battle. Then there would be a resurrection of all souls for a last judgment and consignment to heaven or hell.

The Magi, the three wise men who came from Persia to worship the infant Christ, came to honor the savior, the descendant of Zoroaster.

Historically, the Jewish religion was much less concerned with the hereafter than with the here. The philosopher Moses Maimonides said that it is unrewarding to be concerned with the problem. "Know that just as a blind man can form no idea of colors nor a deaf man comprehend sounds, so bodies cannot comprehend the delights of the soul. And even as fish do not know the element fire because they exist in its opposite, so are the delights of the world of the spirit unknown to this world of flesh."

Jews today hold a wide range of beliefs—from nominal survival of the soul to resurrection to little or no faith in any form of survival after death. Whatever the belief, the emphasis is on living a full life in this world rather than worrying about the next one.

The Jews had been exposed to Zoroastrianism during the Babylonian captivity, and by the time of Christ the dissident Pharisees believed in resurrection. The dominant Sadducees opposed any belief in an afterlife. After the destruction of the Temple in A.D. 70, belief in the resurrection of the body and soul became part of the orthodox Jewish faith. By that time, the apostle Paul was broadcasting the message of a risen Christ and the promise of resurrection through Christianity in the gentile world. Later, resurrection was accepted by Islam after the prophet Muhammad.

Confidence in resurrection and heaven helped people endure suffering in this world, the promise of judgment with just rewards and punishments helped them endure wickedness and unfairness in this life. Christianity became the world's largest religion. Even so, the rise of rationality in the eighteenth century, the ascendancy of science in the nineteenth, and the ever-widening knowledge of how nature works in the twentieth undermined confidence in resurrection and immortality.

By the Middle Ages, people were managing to come to terms with their destiny. They had, in the phrase of the French historian Philippe Ariès, learned to tame death. They met death, in his word, "halfway between passive resignation and mystical trust." Death was a common occurrence to people, present everywhere, the collective destiny: it happened to everyone. It was a familiar experience because, for one thing, the ritual of death was a public ceremony attended by family, friends, acquaintances, and neigh-

bors with their children as well as the clergy. This ceremony—
more important than the funeral and mourning—was organized
by the dying person himself. It was natural for him to know by
some inner conviction that he was going to die. It is a phenomenon that persists to this day, although contemporary people may
wish to ignore the body's harbinger. The medieval person desired
this premonition in order to have time to prepare himself properly
for his leave-taking. And the ritual itself helped to ease the act of
dying.

Lying on his sickbed on his back so that his face was turned
toward heaven, the dying person expressed his sadness for the
end of life, and for the beloved beings and things he was leaving.
After this lamentation, the dying person forgave those in attend-
ance who may have wronged him.

Now it was time to turn away from the world and think of
God. In the first part of his ritual prayer, the dying person con-
fessed his sins. The penitent asked to be admitted to heaven. The
second part of the prayer began, "True Father who never lies,
who recalled Lazarus from the dead, who saved Daniel from the
lions, save my soul from all peril. . . ."

At this point, the priest administered absolution, read psalms,
burned incense, and sprinkled the dying person with holy water.
After the prayer, all that remained was to wait for death, and,
says Ariès, "there was no reason for death to tarry." Whether
death came quickly or slowly, the dying person waited in silence
—he had said his final prayer and spoke no more.

Beginning about A.D. 1100 and through the next three or four
centuries, a slow evolution modified the deathbed scene. The
concept developed that the dying person entered a celestial court
of justice. In scenes of the period, Christ sits upon a judgment
throne surrounded by his court. The dying person's good and bad
deeds are placed on scales; they are also entered in the book of
life. This was a preliminary judgment, for the book remained

open until the Last Judgment and the Second Coming of Jesus at the end of the world. In the meantime, the dying person had this preliminary account book. The common destiny of death was becoming an individual event, and its meaning—whether a transition to heaven or hell—depended upon one's moral and religious record.

By the fifteenth and sixteenth centuries, the court of justice had turned into a trial by temptation. On one side are God, Jesus, the Virgin Mary, and angels; on the other, Satan and his legion of demons. God is there to see how the dying person conducts himself at this final test. The dying person is presented with his entire life as it is recorded in the book. If he is tempted to despair over his sins, to boast over his good deeds or to cling to his love of worldly things, his weakness at this last trial can cancel out all his previous good works and he is lost to the forces of evil. If, on the contrary, he holds fast against these temptations, this final act can erase all his previous sins and he is saved.

From then on, it was commonly believed that a person's entire life flashed before his eyes at the moment of death. It became important to strive for a good death . . . particularly since it could nullify a lifetime of wickedness. And so the act of death itself became a dramatic, emotional, and personal event.

Beginning with the eighteenth century (when rationalism was weakening traditional religious beliefs), death as the familiar common destiny gave way to a new image. Death was a break, a rupture. The event was noteworthy for its own sake, stirring strong emotions. The death of a person wasn't simply his own affair. It was important to survivors, too. The death had an effect on *them* as well. The dying person still presided at his deathbed scene, but now other people were no longer bystanders. They had a role. Sorrow was no longer perfunctory ritual but was deeply felt, and by the nineteenth century grief was being expressed with emotion that verged on hysteria.

Responsibility in the act of dying passed from the dying person himself to those around him, his family and friends. From this grew the impulse in the second half of the nineteenth century to shield the affected person from his plight. This attitude expanded into hiding any strong reaction around the dying person or the bereaved family in order not to add to their burdens. Hush and shush were the bywords.

The ritual of death gradually lost dramatic impact. The occasion was no longer considered a contest for the dying person's soul, and a good many people had doubts whether any kind of existence awaited them after death. Friends and neighbors no longer filed in and out of the death chamber. The public scene changed into a private one. Physicians had determined by this time that it was unsanitary to have all those people in the room. The dying person was sick, obviously. And that led to an obvious conclusion: dying is morbid.

It was but one more step for society to hide the whole ugly scene from view. Strong emotions were to be controlled in public. Why should the discordant note of death intrude upon the rest of society? Dying people were shunned.

By the middle of the twentieth century, no one presided over his death at home, surrounded by family and friends. One went to a hospital to die, alone, surrounded by tubes and life-support machines and strangers. Now a new kind of trial unfolded in the death chamber. The dying person frequently might be unconscious or beyond caring, but a stubborn struggle was fought for his life.

It was a contest between science and death, the enemy.

 THREE

Science Looks at Death

What is death really?

Death, we all know, is the disappearance of life from something that has been living. We don't say that a stone has died or is dead. Instead, we say it is inanimate. A stone and a corpse are not at all alike. For one thing, a corpse could be almost entirely alive.

Let us see how death comes about. The crucial action is loss of oxygen (or some other insult) to the brain. This is usually brought about by a heart stoppage, in which the heart no longer pumps blood with its life-giving oxygen through the circulatory system; but it could also be caused by a clot in an artery preventing blood from reaching the brain, or what we know as a stroke; or by a blow to the head in an automobile accident or a fall that damages the cerebral blood vessels or causes a swelling to squeeze off the blood supply; or by drowning, electrical shock that stops the heart, smothering, choking, emphysema, lung cancer—the list is long.

When heartbeat and breathing stop, death has begun. This is known as clinical death. It is the beginning of the countdown to permanent death. The outstanding characteristic of clinical death is that it is potentially *reversible*. A person can be dead clinically and still return to a normal life if death does not progress beyond this first stage. But something must be done in a hurry.

While blood and oxygen are being denied to tissues throughout the body, the cells most vulnerable to this and all other kinds of injury are in the brain, and in one particular part of the brain: the cerebrum. This prominent front part of the brain that you see in anatomy illustrations (it accounts for 80 percent of the brain material) controls our consciousness and voluntary actions, provides our ability to conceptualize and reason, stores our memories and learning. Without it, we cannot function as waking, purposeful, experiencing beings. So sensitive are these cerebral cells that they begin to show changes in their electrical activity within four seconds after the heart stops pumping blood and their electrical responses stop entirely thirty seconds later. These cells begin to die four to six minutes after being deprived of oxygen. The damage is irreversible because brain cells cannot repair or replace themselves like skin cells.

Therefore, when the heart or breathing stops, medical first-aides have about four minutes to begin artificial respiration, heart massage, or other resuscitation measures that will forestall brain damage. If the lungs and heart can be made to function mechanically to keep oxygen-rich blood nourishing the system, then the brain is preserved intact, also preserving the chance that the person may be able to return to normal life.

The restoring of circulation after the crucial six or so minutes still saves other parts of the brain, those lower centers supervising the involuntary functions that maintain our bodies. This kind of situation comes about in many ways. An automobile accident or some other blow to the head, extremely high fever, or stroke can kill a critical number of cerebral cells while other brain cells survive. The person is able to breathe normally and his heart beats normally, but he is in a coma, unconscious. He is alive, but living on a reduced level of functioning. He can never return to intelligent life. Of course, persons can be rendered unconscious in a coma in various ways that do not include the killing of cerebral cells, and thus many of them can regain consciousness and resume normal lives.

If there is an absence of oxygen for fifteen minutes, the brain dies completely. And with the brain dead, the body's networks— the various organ systems—shut down. For all practical purposes, the person is dead, cannot come back. This is biological death.

But except for the brain the body is still alive, locally. The liver is still making glucose; hair and fingernails will grow for another twenty-four hours; muscles have tone and will react to electrical impulses. If a heart-lung machine pumps oxygenated blood and if glucose is fed intravenously, then death can be kept from spreading further. In fact, this happens in instances where there has been some brain damage, although physicians are not certain how much and may hold out hope for recovery. In cases where there is massive brain damage and obvious brain death, the rest of the body may be preserved temporarily in this manner until the intact heart, kidneys, or other organs can be removed for transplant to another patient.

Without such intervention, other parts of the body begin to break down. Kidneys may keep their normal capacity for thirty minutes to an hour and continue functioning to some extent for two hours, but after one hour the damage is probably irreversible. The situation is comparable for the heart. After about two hours, rigor mortis sets in. Until this time, the muscle cells have retained enough energy to stay relaxed, as resting muscles normally are. But when cellular energy is consumed to a critical level without resupply, the muscle cells are no longer able to maintain the stretched position. They contract, and the body stiffens. Rigor mortis lasts for about thirty hours; then the muscles soften and once again appear to relax. But this time the muscles are dead. What has taken place in the meantime is cellular death.

Living cells harbor within them their own self-destruct mechanisms. This is necessary because after a cell dies in a living person it must be disposed of or else the living body would turn into a dump heap of dead cells that interfered with the living ones. Researchers believe that altered cellular chemistry triggers the rupture of tiny sacs called lysosomes inside the cells. A regiment of enzymes streams out to begin dissolving the cell in a process called autolysis. The process is completed in twenty-four to thirty-six hours in heart, liver, and kidney cells, and, as noted, in about thirty hours in muscle cells. Various enzyme activities in the blood have been observed to peak at thirty-six to forty-eight hours, sixty hours, and eighty hours after brain death.

At the same time, another process of decomposition is under way. Air-breathing organisms invade the body through the respiratory system and begin to attack the tissues. This is a short-term venture, because these bacteria deplete the oxygen as they go along and finally create a situation that cannot sustain them, but that is attractive to organisms that normally live in the in-testines and exist without oxygen. These bacteria migrate through the blood and lymph channels to spread through the tissues. They are the most effective decomposers, but they can be joined at the feast by other scavengers such as fungi and insect larvae. Old stories in the ghostly tradition tell of human remains dug from a grave that glowed with a strange light. We now know that the light comes from bacteria that give off a luminous aura.

And so the processes of death and decomposition proceed, with some tissues yielding more quickly than others. The obvious early changes are the clouding of the cornea of the eyes, the cooling of the body, and the onset of rigor mortis. Later, the release of hemo-globin from red blood cells begins the discoloration of tissues. Gases are produced in the tissues. Blisters develop in the skin. As tissues turn to liquid and gas pressures build, the body swells. The cadaver gives off the characteristic rotten-eggs odor of putrefac-tion. The skin is tinted by blues and reds and dark greens. Dis-colored natural fluids and liquefied tissues, turned to froth by the internal gas pressure, bubble from the nostrils and mouth and ears. The eyes bulge and the swollen tongue protrudes. Skin blisters burst, and finally the bloated body breaks open.

The processes of liquefaction and disintegration continue until

SCIENCE LOOKS AT DEATH   31

only the most resistant tissues remain: hair, nails, eye lens, and cartilage; and finally only teeth, skull, and bones persist in the familiar skeleton.

From this description, it can be seen that dying and death are processes that extend through an unbroken series of transitions from impending death to reversible death to irreversible death to absolute death to disintegration. While an exact moment of death may be assigned to satisfy legal requirements, the designation of such a moment is arbitrary in terms of the natural processes going on in the body. Organs continue to function for hours after the person has died, while the breakdown of tissue is carried out by the same kinds of chemical enzymes that advance the processes of living. Seen in this way, what we call death is the last part of life. Indeed, in the functioning of cells the changeover is so subtle that scientists cannot tell when a cell is dead until they spot a telltale change in structure.

A dramatic example of this principle. In 1974, scientists found bacteria that had been buried in the frozen ground of Antarctica for at least ten thousand years. By the standard of functioning, the organisms were not alive. They had not functioned for ten thousand years. But the cold had preserved intact the structures of these simplest units of life, and under favorable conditions they revived and went on to reproduce colonies of their kind.

If structure changes, function changes or ceases. "Death," says neurosurgeon A. Earl Walker, "is generally considered a structural change resulting in the final and irreversible cessation of function." Essentially, for us, death is the permanent disruption of those brain structures that support the characteristics of the soul or what scientists today call the self.

If death could be distilled to its essence, to one word, what would that word be? Stop a moment and take a guess—because modern biology has supplied an answer to that question. Here's a hint. Try to define the essential quality of life with a single word, for that is the way the scientists went about the problem. What they wanted to know was: What is life?

Not so many years ago, biologists thought they had life pretty well staked out and described . . . so that you could not confuse it with something else. Life, they said, was characterized by organization, metabolism, growth, reproduction, irritability, and adaptation. In a way this was academic because we all know what life is—right?

But as scientific investigators advanced further into the complexities of nature, the more blurred distinctions became. Wendell Stanley, a Nobel biochemist, wrote in 1957:

> One would think that the nature of life would be easy to define, since we are all experiencing it. However, just as life means different things to different people, we find that in reality it is extremely difficult to define just what we mean by life or by a living agent in its most simple form. There is no difficulty in recognizing an agent as living or nonliving as long as we contemplate structures such as man, cats, dogs, or even small organisms such as bacteria or, at the other extreme, structures such as a piece of iron or glass, an atom of hydrogen, or even a molecule of water, sugar, or of our blood pigment, hemoglobin.

The trouble comes when one reaches the frontier of life, where Dr. Stanley had been exploring—with viruses. A virus is a halfway station between the living and nonliving. It is about halfway in size between the smallest living cell and the biggest nonliving molecule. At times the virus is alive, at other times it is not, existing as a nonliving crystal. But, unlike a crystal of salt, a virus comes to life if it finds a congenial environment. Unlike all other living things, it cannot reproduce its kind by itself. A virus must inject its DNA or RNA genetic substance into a cell, whereupon the invading part of the virus commandeers necessary material from the cell to manufacture a brood of new viruses.

"Viruses were discovered by virtue of their ability to replicate, and in the last analysis this ability to reproduce remains today as the only definitive way in which they can be recognized," Stanley concluded. "The essence of life is the ability to reproduce." He went on to say that reproduction is accomplished by using energy to bring random materials from the environment together into a predetermined pattern that will persist through time. "This," said Dr. Stanley, "is life."

However, it was pointed out that fire uses energy and chemicals from its surrounding environment in order to grow and maintain itself. It adapts to environmental conditions and reproduces itself through sparks. We know that fire is not alive, but what is its distinguishing characteristic? Moreover, crystals—nonliving crystals—can both grow and reproduce themselves. True, the growth and reproduction are not accomplished through an internal organization in the fashion of living things, but by adding on externally. Nevertheless, they can grow and reproduce.

Things got to such a state that a physicist at Massachusetts Institute of Technology, Philip Morrison, predicted that in the near future we would create a form of machine life based on computer science and technology. *New York Times* science writer Boyce Rensberger commented on Dr. Morrison's prediction: "To think of a highly complex machine as a form of life is not so unthinkable as it once was for the traditional definitions of life are now quite shaky. . . . The essentials are functions and not forms. If wires and magnets and transistors can be made to function in ways analogous to the function of nerve fibers and protoplasm, are they not just as much alive?"

Another leading scientist, Nobel biologist Jacques Monod of France, tried to show the difference between living things and machines. Dr. Monod conceded it wasn't easy to distinguish between them, because we can build such sophisticated machines these days. Just imagine conversing with a teletype machine that you were not sure was operated by an advanced computer or by a man in another room. If that computer were programmed to respond like a particular man with a certain body of information, it would become tantalizingly difficult to tell whether you were communicating with a machine or a human being.

Well, for one thing, Dr. Monod said, machines cannot build themselves. Living things are self-constructing machines. Living things can grow. However, he admitted, this did not eliminate crystals. Secondly, machines cannot make other machines in their own image. Living things are self-reproducing machines. Again, crystals can reproduce. The third difference makes living things unique from all nonliving things, Dr. Monod said. Machines are made by living things for particular purposes. Living things make themselves—evolve—but their purpose is a result of their development. Function comes from structure. The design of an eye and a camera is similar, so are what they are meant to do and the way they operate—but they were created in two totally different ways.

Obviously, the scientific attempt to separate life and nonlife becomes very difficult. Still, as our common sense tells us, there is a difference between living and nonliving things. Dr. Stanley was close to defining it back in 1957, and would have had it with a shift of emphasis. While he said that reproduction is the one essential characteristic of living things, he added that life has another basic property, although he didn't think it was absolutely necessary. This property is the ability to mutate and preserve the changes through reproduction.

The more scientists thought about this ability to change and keep the change through the generations, the more important it appeared, the more necessary for existence. Essential, really. Any organization that is so locked in, so rigid that it cannot adapt to meet the changing conditions of its environment, is doomed. Flame may grow and reproduce, use energy and materials from the environment, but it cannot modify itself. Neither can crystals mutate and preserve the change in new crystals. When crystals turn into living viruses, they can change into new forms. Flu is caused by a fast-mutating virus, which is why last year's vaccine may be useless for next year's epidemic and why the disease cannot be contained as polio was.

The unique characteristic of life, say modern biologists, is the ability to mutate and preserve the change through reproduction. Nonliving things or systems are immutable. So that is the answer to the original question. Conversely, the essential word for life is: Mutability, the ability to change, to evolve.

We acknowledge as much with the old saying, "Where there is life there is hope." The tragic quality of death is its finality. It is the cut-off. The person has no more chance to do.

By applying this definition to Dr. Morrison's suggestion, we can rule out the construction of a machine that lives. A computer cannot modify itself (or, for that matter, then reproduce a new kind of computer) to adapt to a changing environment.

Mutability fits well with what we know of evolution, which is really a history of life and death on our planet. A cardinal lesson of evolution is that life moves forward intimately related to its environment. They are intertwined, environment shaping life, life modifying environment. The environmental movement of today stems from the concern that we are changing the human environment too quickly and adversely for our own good. To put it plainly, a polluted environment means polluted people. A case in point is the medical belief that perhaps 85 percent of all cancers have environmental triggers.

For years after Darwin published the theory of evolution in 1859, people had the notion that evolution meant law of the fang. "Red in tooth and claw" was the phrase. This interpretation came about because someone said evolution meant survival of the fittest and a lot of other people thought this meant that the most powerful, vicious and heartless critters wiped out the "less fit." This doctrine was perfectly suited for unprincipled captains of industry who cheated customers and employees alike and who ran roughshod over anyone who got in their way. They justified their actions as merely following the law of nature.

The fact is that the most powerful killer that ever stalked the earth—*Tyrannosaurus rex,* the real-life model for Godzilla— didn't make it in nature's sweepstakes. Tyrannosaurus and all the other dinosaur kingpins disappeared about 70 million years ago. Why this happened is one of the great mysteries. One guess is that the climate changed and dinosaurs could not adapt to the change. It must be remembered that they were reptiles and did have handicaps. They were cold-blooded animals; they laid eggs and left them; the newborn and young had to fend for themselves.

On the basis of survival, other kinds of creatures have been more successful. Which living things would you nominate as the most successful? (Do not look at the next line if you wish to guess.)

Honors would have to go to lowly bacteria, one-celled organisms so primitive that they do not readily fit into either the animal or plant kingdom and could be first or second cousins to the first life forms on earth more than 3 billion years ago. A little sea organism with the scientific name of Lingula has existed for 450 million years. And oysters of 150 million years ago have changed so little they would be perfectly acceptable in any seafood restaurant today. In comparison, man has been around for only about 1.5 or 2 million years, and our particular species of *Homo sapiens* —intelligent man—for less than fifty thousand years.

The reason why Lingula, oysters, horseshoe crabs, and other sea creatures have survived virtually unchanged for tremendously long periods of time is that the ocean environment has been so stable. These creatures each successfully filled a niche, or way of life, that was not in direct competition with another kind of creature. And since their marine world didn't change, they didn't have to either. Bacteria are eminently successful in exploiting the world and resources of the very small. Although we human beings are smarter and more powerful than bacteria, we cannot do things that they can do. And while we may be able to sterilize surgical tools and even entire rooms, we could not eliminate bacteria from any significant part of the earth even if we wanted to. They literally flood the earth, its most plenteous life forms.

In contrast to the relatively few stable life forms, most kinds of animals that lived on earth have disappeared. A species can become extinct by turning into something else. Fifty million years ago, Eohippus, the dawn horse, was about the size of a small fox terrier. It browsed on leaves, and had three toes. During 50 million years, the horse kept growing bigger and changing through a series of forms, appearing in a completely new one on the average of once every 6.25 million years. Today, we know, Clydesdale horses can weigh as much as three thousand pounds, all horses are one-toed, and they are grazers of grass and grains. Eohippus is gone, but its descendant, Equus, is very much with us.

Another kind of extinction comes about when the species simply dies out, leaving no descendants. This can happen, as in the probable case of dinosaurs, because the environment changes in some adverse way or too quickly for the doomed species to cope with. Advancing glaciers eliminated many species unable to move to a new habitat.

There is a third way that species have been eliminated, and that is by being replaced by a more successful life form. What happens is not some prehistoric equivalent of the shootout at the OK Corral, but more like the replacement of quill pens by typewriters for writing business letters. There was competition rather than combat for the same set of resources, and the species that did the best job of using the resources to progagate its offspring gradually got to take over that particular sphere of nature. In this sense it *was* "more fit" and thus survived.

When we look at life and death on the grandest scale possible, that of evolution, we come upon a tantalizing contradiction. The individual always disappears, so do species—yet life is immortal. The broad categories of life forms—whether protozoa, worms, insects, mollusks or vertebrates—go on even as the specific models in which life is carried forward die and are remolded with the passage of time.

In the wake of Darwin, all kinds of scientists began investigating evolution, and one of them—a German biologist named August Weismann—made the startling discovery that death is not a necessary part of life. Look at the one-celled bacterium, or amoeba, Weismann said. As long as it has enough food and does not run into some kind of environmental problem, it can go on regenerating forever. It is potentially immortal. Necessarily so, he contended, because if an organism that is entirely contained in one cell lost its vitality and died out after a certain number of reproductions, that would be the end of the strain.

When critics argued that cell division is comparable to death because the original individual disappears, replaced by two new ones, Weismann retorted in the best murder-mystery tradition: If death has occurred, show me the corpse!

The one-celled organism avoids death by remaining eternally young, the ideal of human desires. It divides into two new individuals before the parent has begun to grow old, but this eternal youth is maintained only by the sacrifice of the individual.

In general, multi-celled animals reproduce through the sexual union of two individuals of different sexes. They can pass life on only through their specialized sex cells. The bodily cells cannot renew themselves indefinitely. In time, a sufficient number of them die or deteriorate to the point where a vital function is disrupted and the individual dies.

Does death occur because protoplasm, the living material, is not vital or durable enough—or is death built into the organism?

Is our death programmed into us? This issue has been the source of scientific debate for years. Weismann seemed to argue on both sides of the question. We die because a lifetime of wear and tear finally does us in, he said, but at the same time our deaths serve the purposes of evolution by removing worn-out individuals. A modern authority on evolution, biologist George Gaylord Simpson, says that "inevitable old age and death are implanted in the tissues of individuals."

Other scientists argue that what happens to us when we age and die is the opposite of evolutionary programming. We are like a space probe that has been designed to pass Mars but has no further built-in instructions after that, and no component parts specifically produced to last longer than that voyage. The vehicle will keep going, of course, but the failure rate of its guidance and control mechanisms will increase until the unit finally breaks down.

Be that as it may, there is one big hint that nature has programmed living things. Each kind has a characteristic life span. The more simple the organism, the more exact is the timetable of life. A rotifer is a tiny aquatic animal about the size of a pinhead. Rotifers will live for four days, then produce forty eggs during the next eight days, live six more days, and die on schedule after eighteen days. All rotifers. Development of a human being proceeds on a fairly tight schedule, too—formation of the parts before birth, arrival of teeth, and growth to full stature after. The timing of the end can vary widely, however, although the biblical allotment of seventy or eighty years still characterizes the life span of our species.

As a general rule, life span increases with size. A shrew, about the smallest mammal, lives only about one year. An elephant, the largest land mammal, has been known to live seventy-seven years. Somewhere in the middle, our closest animal relatives, the chimpanzee and gorilla, live a maximum of thirty-nine and thirty-six years.

Surprisingly, a mouse and an elephant each have about the same number of heartbeats in a lifetime: approximately 1 billion. The mouse uses his very quickly, however, and only lives an average of eighteen months. The mouse must expend energy much more rapidly than the elephant. The mouse has an enormous body surface in relation to its tiny bulk, whereas the ratio of the elephant's surface to body size is not so great. This means there is greater opportunity for the mouse's internal heat to escape. And that means the little mouse heart, like a runner on a whirring treadmill, must race just to stay even. So size does have a bearing with warm-blooded animals.

Nevertheless, there are disturbing discrepancies in this rule of thumb. Human beings are the biggest exception of all. We live three times longer than we should according to our place in the scale. Why? scientists wanted to know, but no one could give an answer until about fifteen years ago. Then George Sacher at Argonne National Laboratory discovered that *brain* weight corresponded more closely to life span than body weight. And when he put the two together, he had a still better indicator. His rule is: The bigger the brain in relation to the body, the longer a mammal lives. One reason apparently is that the relatively larger brain system provides greater nerve control of the body's functioning. And so the growth of the human brain to its present size during the last few million years of evolution gave us not only our prized intelligence but the gift of longer life.

It is rare but not unheard of for a human being to live more than a hundred years. About 13,000 Americans are centenarians. That means statistically one chance in about 16,000 to live to be 100 years or older. Few people live beyond 110 years, but in May 1973, the Social Security Administration said it was sending monthly checks to a man in Florida who was 130 years old. And in a part of the Soviet Union known as Abkhazia, an unusual number of people live well beyond a century. Although their ages lack the authentication of birth certificates, a visiting American medical scientist believed that one woman was between 130 and 140 years old.

While these Abkhazian old-timers may enjoy some hereditary advantage, the way they live may be the more important reason for their long lives. They are happy people. They work in the fields, generally, and like what they do. They can keep working as long as they wish, and work as little or as much as they want as they grow older. The continued work helps them to feel important because they are contributing to their community. They also feel important because old people are respected and admired. Each year is an added achievement.

A person born in the United States has a life expectancy of almost 72 years (71.9). A person born in Sweden, the Netherlands, or Norway can expect to live nearly three years longer. People also live longer than Americans in Denmark, Switzerland, Canada, Great Britain, New Zealand, and Australia. These are average ages, of course. If you are born a girl in the United States, your life expectancy is 75.9 years, whereas if you are born a boy it is only 68.2 years—a difference of one-tenth of a lifetime. If you are born white in the United States, your average lifetime is more than 72 years; if you are born black, Hispanic or Indian, it is 65.5 years. If you marry, you have a better chance of living longer than if you stay single or are divorced. You also have a better chance of living longer if you reside in the country rather than in a city.

If you had been born in 1900, your life expectancy would have been only 47 years. The gain of twenty-four years was a result mainly of improved medical and health techniques that conquered most infectious diseases. Most of the gain came from saving people who would have died young, enabling many more people to live to reasonably ripe ages. But when a person reaches age 60, expectancy for his remaining years is about the same as it always was.

The human life span has a recognizable pattern. The pattern's border forms the profile of human death.

The greatest losses occur right at the beginning, in the first three months after conception. About one pregnancy in five aborts spontaneously for a variety of reasons. If the fetus gets beyond the initial hazardous period, its chance to survive gets better. So just being born is an achievement.

But birth itself is a time of danger. One in twenty newborns in the United States is dead at birth or dies during the first year of life. But having survived the first year or two, the child heads into the safest period of the whole life span—the decade between five and fifteen years. The child is protected at home and has none of the responsibilities and risks of adulthood. Experts have figured that if we could stay as free of death as we are at the age of ten, we could live for seven centuries before *half* of us died.

By the age of ten or eleven, most children have gained a full understanding about death, that it is final and inevitable and will happen to them. The child's discovery of death parallels or recapitulates the racial discovery of death. We come into the world believing we are immortal, and we must learn otherwise. Freud tells us that the unconscious, that part of the mind that is most basic and that houses our instincts and never comes into contact with outside reality, believes it is immortal. That is why, even as adults, we have the feeling that we will go on forever, that death is for other people. It takes an act of conscious intellect to remind ourselves that no one is exempt. Similarly, it is difficult if not impossible to visualize one's own death. If you think about your death, it is from the point of view of another person, who observes your corpse and who, obviously, still lives.

Most psychologists say that during the first two years of life a baby has no conception of death. But even a child that young probably comes into contact with ideas that are the basis for the concepts of being and nonbeing. Sleep is a strong model of death for a child. The interlinking of the two is emphasized in a prayer commonly taught to children:

> Now I lay me down to sleep,
> I pray the Lord my soul to keep;
> And if I die before I wake,
> I pray the Lord my soul to take.

The infant delights in the game of peekaboo, the disappearance and reappearance of another person. The term peekaboo comes from Old English words meaning "Alive or dead?" Even very young children get an idea of separation and loss when their mother does not appear when she is supposed to.

Indeed, at the age of about three years, when a child begins to grasp some idea of death, it is equated with separation. Grandpa is dead. He has gone to sleep or gone away. Conversely, the prospect of a separation from a parent can arouse strong fears because a child cannot tell the difference between a short-term departure and death. The child from three to five years still does not understand death as final. Grandpa has gone away. When is he coming back?

The young child also does not understand that death is inevitable, probably the most persistent of the childhood attitudes. He is likely to believe that death only happens by accident or when it is produced by some agent. The man is dead because he got "runned over" or because he went into a hospital. From this, the youngster deduces that it is a good idea not to get hit by a car and to stay away from hospitals. His defenses are bolstered by the assumption that death will not happen to him. After all, he is not old or chronically sick and has no intentions of getting into either of those conditions. Associating death only with some obvious cause, children often develop a great fear of murder.

Starting at about age five, a child begins the long accommodation to the idea that death is final, inevitable, and universal. For the first several years of this transition, the child resists accepting death as personal. It is remote, he feels, in terms of his own life. He is caught between contradictory attitudes where he will neither deny nor accept the certainty of his death. He is likely to think of death as a person who comes for you, a bogeyman or skeleton—a figure to be avoided. By the age of ten or eleven, the conflict has usually been resolved and his own death accepted. Of course, death *is* relatively remote for the ten-year-old. It is the safest time of his life span. But we can't remain children forever.

The adolescent's sexual apparatus is the last of the bodily systems to mature, and new emotions run strong. He or she begins to go out into the world, starts to drive a car, leaves home for the first time . . . and begins to die in growing numbers. The death rate climbs sharply until the twenties and then levels off somewhat.

People twenty-five years old are at their physical peak. This conclusion is based on tests of flexibility, agility, strength, endurance, and similar traits. These physical blessings fade little during the twenties, the decade of our physical prime. But scientists believe that after about age thirty our bodily functions begin to decline at a rate of 1 percent a year. This drop-off varies with individuals and with different organ systems. The early physical losses are hardly noticed, if at all, for nature endows us with far greater capacity than we need. After all, a person can live with one lung, part of one kidney, a fraction of his intestines.

Most people coast through their thirties cushioned by the margin of safety built into their bodies. After about age forty, specific ailments begin to surface in less-favored people. Entering the second half of adulthood, people die at an increasing rate. The number of deaths doubles about every eight years of advancing age. This escalation applies to all societies, rich or poor, advanced or primitive. The same rate of death was found to apply to white laboratory rats and to fruit flies. It seems to be universal with living systems. It means that the chances of dying at age eighty-five are a hundred times greater than they are at age thirty-five.

There comes a point in the later stages of adulthood when physical declines are no longer masked. They are evident in physique, figure, and faces; in the eyeglasses needed for reading. One of the things that have been happening over the years is that the body's collagen—protein that fills in cracks and cavities like stuffing—grows more rigid. One reason a baby is so rubbery is that the collagen's fibers are distributed in random fashion. But the longer we live, the more these fibers tend to line up like files of soldiers in regimental review. With collagen making up one-third of all protein, the body loses its elasticity. So does the lens of the eye. By the mid-forties, the lens can't bend as it once did to focus on close objects, and people of this age have difficulty reading small print.

The way we think also tends to become more structured as we go along. This is almost unavoidable, because each of us must live his or her own life in a particular way, through a certain period, employed in a specific kind of occupation. Because of their experiences and the structures of their thinking, it is unlikely that a painter, an ecologist, and a lumberman will regard a forest in the same way. It is not by accident that inventions and poetry are created by young minds, while philosophers, leaders of church and state—people who use accumulated knowledge and experience—exist at the other end of the life span.

Loss of flexibility or adaptability is one of the prime characteristics of aging. Although scientists know a great deal about the subject, they still do not know exactly what aging is or what causes it. They do not consider it a disease, although a person's susceptibility to disease increases as he grows older. Molecular biologists may decipher the secret as they learn the language of life written in the genetic code in our cells. In the meantime, growing old and experiencing old age await everyone who succeeds in living long enough. In American society, unlike that of

Abkhazia, the last stage of life is looked upon with mixed feelings.

By this time, the tempo of a person's life is usually slowing, its scope contracting. Children are grown, away from home, beginning their own lives, so parents no longer enjoy the central roles they once did. At work, the breadwinner may find he is being bypassed, being "put on a shelf." His last years on the job may be a marking of time. At sixty-five, most people must retire. At sixty-five, a person becomes officially old. Retirement usually means a reduced income and less buying power. That often means a reduced status in the community. Health problems now become more vexing. Reduced health curtails activities that may have given pleasure for years. The elderly person's mobility is curtailed as well. Friends die, others are too far away to visit. If the aged person cannot function independently and has no family able or willing to take care of him, he will probably be confined to a nursing home. A person's self-esteem can fall before such an assault, leading him to think of himself as no longer valuable. Under these circumstances, it may require a strong will or an optimistic outlook to sustain a zest for living.

In America, old age is looked upon as a prelude to death. A society that denies death does not want to be reminded of it by old age.

 FOUR

Invisible Death

How can a society "deny" something so universal as death? That's impossible, you say—ridiculous! And besides, you ask on second thought, is it true? Don't we see death all the time on television? Isn't one of the main criticisms of TV programming that there is an obsession with death and violence?

It is true that a great number of prime-time TV entertainment programs feature crime, and violence is the device used to snare audience interest. The program usually begins with a murder. That event gets the story rolling and motivates the hero to track down the murderer. Along the way, we can expect several more homicides—bystanders who get in the way of a crime or other victims of the criminal as he tries to avoid capture. At the end, the chase. Police cars, sirens blaring, pursue the villain, demolishing other automobiles along the way. The stealthy approach to the cornered murderer. The shootout, and the culprit is killed or caught.

We turn off the set grateful for the hour or two of suspense that allowed us to escape from the routine problems of life. Everybody —at least a mass audience—loves a gunfight, the TV producers say, and add: People know it is only fiction.

So is *Our Town,* a play by Thornton Wilder, only fiction. The play concerns a town in New England at the beginning of the century, an ordinary town with ordinary people. People who remind you of yourself and those around you. No blur of motion, no speeding automobiles through scenic, authentic locales. The play takes place on a bare stage and your imagination fills in what is necessary. Gradually, you become involved with two families concerned with the problems and events of growing up and growing old. A father reprimands a teen-age son for not helping his mother more with the chores. A daughter looks back lovingly on her twelfth birthday with her family. The boy and girl fall in love and decide to marry.

Later, we discover she has died in childbirth. We see the young man, now a widower, at the cemetery, devastated. Shattered by grief and desolation, he comes back at night after the funeral and falls across her new grave. Our hearts go out to him in his pain. Our hearts go out to her, that the carrier of life should be taken. The loss! The irreparable loss! She condemned to die, he to live without her. That nature can be so kind to us and so cruel! This is death.

And only fiction.

What is the difference between *Our Town* and the TV series? On the TV program, the people who die are practically anonymous. We have never seen the murdered store owner before— never saw him alive—or the pedestrians who got shot during the holdup in progress. Even if the victim is given more importance in the plot, he is presented with no past and little present. His life has no meaning for us and so neither does his death. We are held by whatever gruesome means of killing the scriptwriter can concoct, captives of the action and the unraveling of plot. We watch with dry eyes. We see death, but we are insulated from it.

There is another, perhaps thicker layer to the shield. The TV programs imply that the *only* way people die is through violence. This has raised public fears of violence, but it is consistent with our unconscious belief that we ourselves are immortal and death only happens to somebody else. It reaffirms the childish attitude that death is inflicted only by accident or by some unusual agent. It does not happen to everyone, only the luckless few. If we look further back into the human past, we can see the ancient belief that death never comes naturally but is caused through the magic of an evil person or spirit.

Undoubtedly these buried attitudes strengthen the appeal of these programs. And undoubtedly no one could endure spending every night in front of the TV set racked by grief at a truly-felt death. As the TV programmers say, they are merely giving the public what it wants. It is a two-way contract.

That is the point. We don't want to be exposed to death.

There is another public demand that television programs dutifully supply. The happy ending. No matter what the perils or complications, everything comes out for the best. The happy ending is a denial of the ultimate ending. It ignores or covers up what we know must be the true ending of our lives. When this format is joined with the popular medical story, we are misled in still another way. The hero-physician always triumphs in the end, the sickness is cured, the victim is saved. Repeated doses of this myth, reinforced by news stories from time to time of medical accomplishments in real life, give rise to an impression that medical science and doctors are omnipotent. It comes as a distinct shock to learn that someone you love in these advanced times has a fatal disease. It is an outrageous, unacceptable condition, and when one finds it one is tempted to look for some supposed medical negligence that allowed it to happen.

Now, happy endings, cops and robbers, cowboys and bad guys, "whodunits" are standard forms of entertainment. People have reveled in fictional gore and thrilled to fictional horrors for a long time. But it is one thing to read of these things on the printed page and quite another to see and hear them—a steady barrage of them—on a TV screen. It is hard to resist the belief that whatever one sees on television is reality.

And part of the time it is. TV news programs do show store

owners who have been killed in holdups or pedestrians gunned down in the crossfire between cops and robbers. We have seen dead bodies in Vietnam and the Middle East. But, again, all of these people are far removed from us and anonymous. And, again, they are mostly victims of random violence or war. Also, we get the fact of death in terms of neutral numbers. And in snippets. "Twelve persons died today when a nursing home burned to the ground in. . . ." "An earthquake in Iran has taken the lives of 452 villagers. . . ." "A man with a rifle went berserk in midtown Detroit. . . ." When a public figure—someone we know—dies, the announcement may be accompanied by an obituary of newsreel clips, a quick series of public scenes to summarize his life. Television news does not have time to do more. It is a capsule front page and is forced to summarize news items. But the effect of these techniques is to keep death remote and impersonal.

It is understandably rare for a news camera crew to be at the scene of death, but it happens occasionally at a disaster. If a reporter comes upon a mother whose child was just killed at a crossing, for example, should he record her wild grief? Apart from charges of sensationalism, questions have been raised over such reporting. How far does a reporter have the right to go to provoke this kind of reaction? Is it humane to record the distraught person at that moment? Is it an intrusion upon her right to privacy? Is it news or should only the circumstances of the death be reported? If it is a legitimate part of the story, when does it become sensationalism? How much should be used? But the big question is: How much does the audience at home eating dinner have stomach for?

Usually the goriest shots are edited out of such incidents before broadcasting them. In the 1975 teleplay *Eric,* about a teen-aged boy dying from leukemia, the youth was shown as fresh-cheeked to the end, even though in actuality leukemia is a wasting and debilitating disease. If a spot news film or videotape of raw grief is used, television viewers will identify with the plight of the victim and bereaved survivors, but, again, these people are anonymous—unknown the moment before and soon to be replaced by another subject. The viewers' momentary distress is dissolved by the next distractions that fly through the television window.

On three occasions—the assassinations of President John Kennedy in 1963, and the Reverend Martin Luther King, Jr., and Senator Robert Kennedy in 1968—the public figures were known to and had deep meaning for millions of people. Their tragic deaths broke through all public defenses to provoke rare, sustained outpourings of grief.

During the years after World War II, the United States became "youth oriented." An adolescent, an uncompleted adult of inferior social status, became a teen-ager: a new market target for commercial entrepreneurs. And, with the help of advertising's time-tested techniques of using bathing beauties to sell products, the nation doted on youth, vitality, and sex appeal. There is nothing wrong with youth, but it is necessary to be aware that this single-minded concentration on one small part of the life span is also a way to avoid unpleasant thoughts about other aspects of the human condition.

Another way to hide death is through the selective use of words. Language is so meshed with our development as human beings and we are so disposed to accept symbols for actuality that words for us can be more powerful than life. Shakespeare's words spoken by Romeo and Juliet can dwarf our own real-life loves. "Give me liberty," said Patrick Henry, "or give me death." Blunt, direct words. Everyone knew where Patrick Henry stood, and colonists responded to this outspokenness. Just as the people in France rallied to the ideal epitomized in the slogan of the French Revolution: "Liberty, Equality, Fraternity."

Given this power of words, the problem becomes how to talk

about death without evoking its terrors—how to take the sting out of death. Two tricks were put into the service of this goal. Several centuries ago, writers and orators decided they could improve what they had to say by making it more flowery. Instead of saying drably that a man drowned, they thought it was more artistic to say that he went to Davy Jones' locker. If a fellow partygoer drank too much wine, only a lout would say that he got drunk. The literary connoisseur said that he imbibed too much of the grape. After a couple of centuries, "imbibing the grape" became tiresome and most people stopped using such artificial phrases, but circumlocution—that is, pussyfooting around the outskirts of a subject to make a point—still meets a social need. We say we are "going to the bathroom" when we mean something more explicit. And when we say a dog is "doing his duty," we don't mean the same thing as when a soldier is doing his.

The second device is known as euphemism. This is the deliberate effort to pull the teeth of a blunt, explicit word by replacing it with a milder substitute. Often this can be done by using technical and Latin-based words. If we say we have to urinate or defecate, we are being more precise than "going to the bathroom" and yet the words still can be used in some social circumstances. Yet those Latinate words do not summon the repugnant images aroused by the short Anglo-Saxon words that society does not want used. Similarly, we do not like to call people poor, because we fear it would offend them or appear to be a snobbish social judgment. Instead, public statements refer to the underprivileged. Poorly skilled workers are underemployed. And poor or backward nations are underdeveloped. In these instances, words that are more generalized, vague, and technical serve the purpose.

Death is a subject that has inspired euphemism. Think of the euphemisms and circumlocutions you have heard used in your own experience. Passed on, passed away, departed, is sleeping, eternal sleep or rest, expired, cut down by the Grim Reaper, deceased, shuffled off this mortal coil, went home, returned to dust, laid down his life, went on to glory, gave up the ghost, snuffed out (like a candle), fell asleep, joined his ancestors, went the way of all flesh, stepped off the deep end, made the supreme sacrifice, came to an untimely end, left us, gained his release, was called home.

You can probably add others. The arsenal of defense words is well stocked.

There is an even more obvious way to deny the existence of death. Simply don't talk about it, particularly in front of children. In August 1970, the magazine *Psychology Today* conducted a poll on attitudes toward death and thirty thousand readers answered questionnaires. One third of those responding could not recall a single instance in childhood when death was discussed within the family. More than another third said the subject was brought up only with discomfort. Three in ten families discussed death openly.

Americans refuse to talk about death, said one minister, the way Victorians refused to talk about sex. Not only is the rule "speak no death, hear no death," but the past several generations of American children have seen no death in the home. The removal of the dying to hospitals, where children under sixteen are usually not allowed, was probably the most important move in completing the isolation of death. Until the last forty years or so, all the generations of children through history grew up with a physical association with death. Because infectious disease was rampant through all those centuries, the death of a brother or sister or even a parent at an early age was commonplace.

According to the *Psychology Today* questionnaire, the first close involvement for more than four in ten people came with the death of a grandparent while for nearly another two in ten it was the death of an animal. Often enough in our mobile society, grandparents die far away, having moved to Florida or some other retirement settlement.

The dramatic elimination of so many deaths at an early age is the result of successful medical and health practices, and nobody would want to return to the old ways. But it is necessary to see how radically our experience has changed if we are to understand what is happening to us.

For example, the idolatry of youth and consequent devaluing of the elderly has had very real effects. The aged person now must deal with a variety of social discriminations that affect his well-being and his own estimate of himself. The vile treatment of elderly people in some nursing homes is one of the ugliest forms this discrimination has taken. The shunning of the terminally ill is another.

This abandonment is no longer limited to the aged. There is a strong tendency today for a young person with a terminal illness to be ostracized by his contemporaries.

Young people's attitudes didn't just get this way, of course. They were cultivated by adult society and with the best intentions: to spare the child. This was brought about not only by hiding the subject of death and isolating the child from it, but by misrepresenting it, sugarcoating it. In reviewing a number of children's books on death in the *New York Times Book Review*, Sheila Cole wrote in September 1971 that all the books intend

> to give a child a way of looking at death and living with the knowledge of it. All of them try to diffuse the finality and fearfulness by presenting death as just another natural process. But to most adults in our culture, death is more than just another natural process. It is an occasion surrounded with mystery and deep emotions. Presenting it to a child as just another change we go through is less than candid. Adults often present a prettier reality to children than actually exists. But to give easy answers to a child's questions about death is to deny reality and to diminish both life and death and ultimately to turn our children from our counsel.

Howard Hoyt, who writes children's stories, wrote this parody:

When little Jane's Auntie Sue died, her mother took her to the funeral parlor for the viewing.

"See all the nice posies?" said her mother. "Those are roses, and those are carnations, and those are hyacinths. Don't they smell just lovely!"

Jane had never seen so many beautiful flowers. She clapped her little hands with glee.

"Why are the people whispering and mumbling?" asked Jane.

"That's to show their respect for Auntie Sue," said her mother.

"But she can't hear them anyhow, can she?" asked Jane.

"No Dear," said her mother, "but isn't that low hum of voices soothing? Don't you love it? Now let's go up and pay our respects to Auntie Sue."

They got in line, and when it was their turn to look, her mother held Jane up to see the pretty coffin. There lay Auntie Sue in her best dress, her hands folded, her eyes closed, snuggling down into the soft creamy satin.

"Doesn't she look wonderful!" said their friend, Mrs. Bradshaw.

"Yes, doesn't she," agreed Jane's mother. "Those two weeks in Arizona did her a world of good."

"And so natural!" added Mrs. Bradshaw.

"Her cheeks look kind of pink," said Jane.

"Mr. Mortimer, the mortician, used cosmetics on Auntie Sue, Dear," explained her mother, "just like you do sometimes with your Barbie doll. Now, isn't this fun?"

[The next day Jane went with her mother and father to the funeral. After the burial, everyone returned to Auntie Sue's and Uncle Ben's for dinner.]

Neighbors had brought in all kinds of cold cuts and potato salad and deviled eggs and pickles and olives and pie and cake. It was just like a picnic except it was inside and they had no three-legged races. Jane never ate so much in her life.

"Have you had a good time, Dear?" asked her mother.

Jane looked at her mother very seriously and thoughtfully. Then her face lit up with a happy, happy smile.

"When are you going to die, Mumsie?"

The extent to which the denial of death had reached—and the fantasies such an attitude can encourage—are contained in a book addressed not to children but adults. The book begins: "Death is an imposition on the human race, and no longer acceptable. Man has all but lost his ability to accommodate himself to personal extinction; he must now proceed physically to overcome it." The book, *The Immortalist,* written by Alan Harrington in 1969, helped to inspire a small cult of "immortalists" dedicated to the goal of getting rid of death by living indefinitely.

There is nothing new in this hope. The search for biological immortality goes back a long time in human affairs. By at least 200 B.C., alchemists in China were engaged in a systematic search for eternal life. It is fascinating that Chinese alchemists, just like those in the West beginning some two centuries later, were preoccupied with gold as the means to their goal. Why was this so?

Have you ever wondered why human beings place such value on gold? The metal is attractive-looking, it is true, and has the malleability to be molded into beautiful jewelry and ornaments. But what about all those gold bricks in Fort Knox that no one sees but that are a foundation of our banks and money?

The value of the precious metal stems from a reason that modern people have forgotten. Primitive human beings divined that the sun is the fountainhead of life. The sun god was worshiped in many religions. In the logic of primitive thinking, if the sun was the source, then the golden radiance, sunshine, was the quintessence of life coming to earth. (As we know today, they weren't far off, since the sun's radiant energy is the source or basis for life on earth.) When gold was first discovered in Nubia south of Egypt about 3500 B.C., it was considered a piece of the sun. It was God brought down to earth, the immortal essence materialized. Pharaohs were buried in gold coffins because that was the fitting substance for their immortal voyages after death. In our own language, the words "god" and "gold" are separated by a single letter.

In time, round gold coins became small replicas of the most important heavenly sphere. Silver and silver coins took their place as second in importance to gold, as the moon is to the sun.

When Western alchemists sought to transmute lead and other "base" metals into gold, they thought they could find in the process the principle or quintessence of immortality. Gradually, gold became valuable not as a holy but as a worldly metal. Kings and princes sought alchemists to manufacture treasure. This demand lured fakers who passed off brass and anything else that looked yellow. Greedy sovereigns became irate at this practice and took to punishing such frauds with execution. One prince, Frederick of Würzburg, built a special gallows—painted gold—just to hang his false alchemists.

In China, alchemists kept seeking the essence of gold as a means to achieve eternal life. They or their royal clients ate with golden utensils, drank from golden goblets, and even sipped gold-tinctured potions in their quest for immortality.

In succeeding centuries, Taoist cultists devoted all their time to the attempt to become immortal. One part of their strategy is a beautiful example of imitative magic. The hopefuls reasoned that the way to live forever was to return to the state of the embryo, the way human life starts out. An embryo does not eat and it does not breathe, and so these would-be immortal saints-in-training practiced eating as little as possible and learning to hold their breath. The trainee started out by practicing to hold his breath for a period of time equal to three, five, seven, and nine normal respirations. When he could hold his breath for a period equivalent to twelve respirations, he had completed a "small series." From there, he had to learn to add one small series to another until he had not breathed for the equivalent of one hundred and twenty normal respirations, a "large series."

The cultist believed that this accomplishment brought a definite improvement in his health. His hands and feet tingled, his face was flushed, and he experienced a delightful intoxication. We know today he was experiencing anoxia, oxygen starvation of the brain. Pilots flying at high altitude have been taught that this sensation of ecstasy is a sign that they have lost their oxygen supply and must do something about it at once. In the case of the Taoist, if he persevered in holding his breath, he would become unconscious and resume breathing.

About the time that alchemy was beginning to turn into the science of chemistry in Europe, Ponce de León was searching in the New World for the fountain of youth. That was another human hope for a while—that such a fountain really existed somewhere, and the real problem was to find it. So the sixteenth-century Spanish adventurer's efforts were given thoughtful attention in some European courts. Ponce de León never found the fountain, of course, but he did discover Florida, where aged people still go, some of them in search of their lost youth.

A hope of today's immortalists is cryonics, a deep-freeze strategy proposed by physicist Robert Ettinger in his 1964 book, *The Prospect of Immortality*. He begins his book: "Most of us now living have a chance for personal, physical immortality." Dr. Ettinger said his case rests on one fact and one assumption.

> *The fact:* At very low temperatures it is possible, *right now,* to preserve dead people with essentially no deterioration, indefinitely.
>
> *The assumption:* If civilization endures, medical science should *eventually* be able to repair almost any damage to the human body, including freezing damage and senile debility or other cause of death.

The strategy, then, is to preserve the structure until function can be restored at some later time. The method would seem to stand a better chance of success if the person could be frozen *before* he died of his fatal natural ailment. In that way, the chance of keeping the brain cells intact would be better. But such an action would be homicide and is prohibited by law. So the cryonics technicians can only begin cooling the candidate for immortality after clinical death and, as we have seen, there remains a scant four to six minutes before cerebral death. Whether this advanced stage of death can be averted is extremely unlikely.

The blood of the "freezee" is replaced with a chemical and is then placed inside a capsule in which the temperature is reduced by liquid nitrogen to 320 degrees below zero. The body can be preserved indefinitely with a maintenance fee of about $1,000 a year.

Researchers at Emory University in Atlanta, Georgia, have reduced the body temperature of dogs from 98 degrees to 40 degrees Fahrenheit. At that point, the animals are clinically dead, with no blood pressure, blood circulation, or electrical activity in the brain. After two hours, the dogs' temperatures have been brought back to normal and the animals have returned to life with no damage. And, of course, there is the recent case of the ten-thousand-year-old bacteria in Antarctica coming back to life.

But the clinical deaths of the dogs were produced by freezing, not other causes. Functioning stopped when the temperature reached 40 degrees. A bacterium cell is radically different from a human being with 80 trillion—that's 80,000,000,000,000—cells. An expert in cryobiology, the scientific study of life at low temperature, points out that while sperm cells have been successfully stored and used later to create human beings, as many as half of these frozen cells die. Professor J. K. Sherman of the University of Arkansas School of Medicine says the variety of human cells (there are about a hundred types) with their different sensitivities to stress makes the prospect of immortality by this method little more than a dream. Not only do we have little knowledge of what low temperatures do to biological systems, but the literature of the Cryonics Society of New York admits: "At present, it is necessary to use unperfected freezing techniques after the patient has been pronounced 'dead' by a physician."

Still, about two dozen people have been deep-frozen by the Cryonics Society of California and several others in New York. Guy de la Poterie of Montreal, father of an eight-year-old girl who died from a kidney ailment and whose body was put in cryonic suspension in Los Angeles, said, "Personally, I have a feeling that science will be able to do something. I'm trying to be realistic about this, but I sincerely think one day they'll be able to revive her. When, I don't know." At the funeral service for cryonically suspended twenty-four-year-old Steven Jay Mandell at St. James, Long Island, the rabbi observed for the first time in his experience no tears, no grief. Steven's mother said, "I think there's so much less of a feeling of loss than in the normal situation, especially where there is a flicker of hope."

Cryonics, then, is changing the old saying. Even where there is death, there is hope.

The objective of immortalists was stated by F. M. Esfandiary, who teaches philosophy at the New School for Social Research in New York City. He said that "death is an end. There is no paradise, no heaven, hell, or reincarnated life. Death therefore is a greater tragedy now than ever before." So: "If dying is natural, then the hell with the tyranny of nature. Why be resigned to it? Let us continue to rise above nature." In short, let us eliminate physical death. Can denial of death be carried any further than that? Or, to put it another way, isn't that conclusion the last logical step for denial-of-death thinking to reach?

Is there anything wrong with this kind of thinking? After all, why not think positively, optimistically. Nothing is wrong as long as what we imagine to be so does not stray from what actually is so. It is only by keeping our thoughts aligned with reality that we can perform effectively.

Often it is the peculiar vision of the artist that first perceives the meaning in a course of events. He interprets his discovery for us in his own medium. Such was the case, we can now see with hindsight, when William Faulkner wrote the short story "A Rose for Emily" in 1930.

The story begins with the death of Emily Grierson. The townspeople go to her funeral, the men out of respect for the end of a tradition—she was the last of the Griersons in their town—and the women out of curiosity to see the inside of the decaying house. No one had visited the house for years. Miss Emily's father drove away her suitors with a horsewhip. She never married, and when he died many years earlier, rumors got about that she was left penniless except for the house. That's when people first began feeling sorry for her.

The day after her father died, a group of ladies called at the Grierson house. Miss Emily was dressed as usual and showed no grief. She told the ladies that her father had not died. For three days she denied to ministers and doctors wanting to bury the body that her father was dead. Then she broke down and let them bury her father.

She was sick for a long time, and when next the town saw her, she had a serene, angelic quality. A construction crew came to town to lay sidewalks, and after a while Miss Emily was seen to take Sunday-afternoon buggy rides with the construction foreman, a northerner named Homer Barron. Soon the town was gossiping about Miss Emily and her sweetheart, with many people maintaining that no Grierson would marry a Yankee.

But, as usual, Miss Emily held her head high and stared down all the talk. That was her way, just like the time she went to the druggist and said she wanted poison. He asked her what for, but all she would say was that she wanted poison, the best. When he pointed out that by law he had to ask her what she wanted the poison for, she simply repeated her demand and stared at him. Finally, the druggist sent her arsenic with the words written on the box: For Rats.

Then townspeople thought she would kill herself. While she was still seeing Homer Barron, he had let it be known to his drinking companions that he was not a marrying man. Still, the town thought that Miss Emily and Homer Barron would get married after she ordered a man's silver toilet set with the initials H. B. on each piece and a complete outfit of men's clothing, including a nightshirt.

Homer Barron was seen entering the kitchen door of Miss Emily's house one evening. But that was the last anyone saw of him. And of her, too, for about six months. She remained inside her house all that time. And when she finally came out again, she had grown fat and her hair was turning gray. It turned quickly to an iron gray, which it remained for the rest of her life. She spent her last years inside the house as a recluse.

And so when Miss Emily died at the age of seventy-four, people were curious about her house. They knew there was one room upstairs that nobody had seen for forty years. They waited until after the burial and then broke down the door to the sealed chamber. The dusty room was furnished like a bridal chamber. On the dressing table were a man's toilet articles tarnished black.

The man himself lay in the bed.

For a long while we just stood there, looking down at the profound and fleshless grin. The body had apparently once lain in the attitude of an embrace, but now the long sleep that outlasts love, that conquers even the grimace of love, had cuckolded him. What was left of him, rotted beneath what was left of the nightshirt, had become inextricable from the bed in which he lay; and upon him and upon the pillow beside him lay that even coating of the patient and biding dust.

Then we noticed that in the second pillow was the indentation of a head. One of us lifted something from it, and leaning forward, that faint and invisible dust dry and acrid in the nostrils, we saw a long strand of iron-gray hair.

 FIVE

Reviving Death

Believing that the conspiracy to conceal death was an unhealthy development, a few people beginning in the 1960s tried to tear down the wall.

The first efforts to make death visible again were directed mainly at professionals who must deal with death. Beginning in the 1970s, these efforts gained momentum and began spreading to other people as well. The attempt to pierce the mass conspiracy was like breaking into a sealed compartment to ventilate its dark and festering interior.

Surprisingly at first thought—but less so as one thinks about it —researchers discovered that headquarters for the conspiracy was the hospital. And among the chief deniers of death were physicians. The reason this information comes as a surprise is that traditionally we think of a hospital as the place where lives are saved. And, of course, they are. But as we noted, in recent years hospitals have also become the place where most Americans die.

As for doctors, a subtle change came to their profession as well. Traditionally, they have been healers. Traditionally, they battled disease, wounds, injuries in restoring health. With today's powerful medical weapons and the physician's new skills and knowledge winning so many of these battles, it becomes easy enough to consider death itself as the enemy. But as soon as a doctor makes

63

that transfer in his mind, he has entered into an impossible contest. One he cannot win.

But our society wants winners. It does not tolerate failure. Losers get lost. This put the physician in an uncomfortable position. He began to regard the death of a patient as his professional failure. Subconsciously, he felt guilty.

One of the pioneers in directing attention to death, a psychiatrist, Herman Feifel, said physicians have "significantly stronger death fears than do most other persons." Another psychiatrist, David Peretz, described the pronounced reactions of medical students confronted with cadavers in the anatomy room. "Some students become depressed; some display grisly humor; some displace their rage at death onto their partners at the table; some drop out of school; some let their partners do the work while they learn just enough to get by, studying the illustrated text and preferring the disembodied illustrations to the real thing."

Researchers found tremendous resistance among doctors to telling patients they were sick with a fatal disease. Surveys showed that up to 90 percent of the doctors interviewed opposed giving terminal patients an honest estimate of their condition, although there are indications that this attitude may be changing among new, young physicians. There were several good reasons for this attitude. For one thing, no patient should be left without hope. The patient needs hope to rally his forces to fight his disease. The will to live is a key element in the struggle.

Furthermore, no one can predict with absolute certainty that a patient has three or six months to live. There have been enough cases of spontaneous remissions in cancer or unexpectedly long survivals with other diseases to remove the absoluteness from such predictions. Also, where chronic kidney diseases may have been fatal a few years ago, now we have dialysis and transplants. There is always the possibility that some new cure may intervene. So, as long as there is life, there *is* reason to hope.

While these are legitimate grounds for wanting to shield the patient, they do not explain the changed behavior of many physicians (documented by investigators) toward terminal patients. These physicians had a tendency to "distance" themselves from terminal patients. The doctors would dash in and out of the room, hardly stopping at the bedside. The doctor would appear too busy to answer the patient's questions or, when he did answer them, reply in incomprehensible medical jargon. As one patient put it, it is difficult to speak to the doctor when he sticks a thermometer into your mouth the moment he comes into the room.

This conspiracy of silence included the nurses and, of course, the visitors to the patient as well. One study found that nurses did not answer calls of terminal patients as quickly as they did the other calls. The nurses weren't acting from heartlessness; rather they tended to "write off" the dying patients, and allocated more of their time to those patients with better chances to survive.

Nevertheless, the effects of the nurses' reasoned behavior can be harsh on the dying. Dr. Elisabeth Kübler-Ross told the U.S. Senate's Special Committee on Aging about a twenty-one-year-old woman suffering from acute leukemia. The girl was full of life and hoped—even though she knew her chances were one in a million—to graduate from college the coming June and get married in July. She went home from the hospital to pursue her dream.

She came back into the hospital five weeks later, again because the family could not get enough home care for her. Her biggest dream was to live at home. She was put into an intensive care unit. When I visited her on New Year's Eve, she was a picture of utter isolation, loneliness, and anguish. I came into the intensive care unit. She was lying there with tubes hanging out of her mouth, her lips cut, the infusion bottle going, a tracheotomy and the respirator, and she was desperately holding my hand.

I covered her with a bed sheet. (She was not even covered.) A nurse came and said: "Don't bother. She is going to push it off anyway." I walked toward her, and she grabbed my hands, pointing her fingers to the ceiling. I looked up and said, "Susie, I think this light bothers you. You are lying on your back and must stare into this light." She grabbed my hands and kissed them, obviously conveying "You are understanding me." I went to ask if these lights could be turned down, only to get a nice lecture about the rules and regulations of the intensive care unit.

I also asked for two chairs for the mother and father to sit down when they visit, because I cannot comprehend why patients have to die alone in an intensive care unit and their families sit alone outside in a waiting room. I was told the mother cannot get a chair because "she stayed more than five minutes last time."

Dr. Ross is one of the chief architects of the campaign to educate people about death. She had a new staff position as a psychiatrist with a hospital in Chicago when she was approached by four theology students in the fall of 1965. They had to write a paper on "crisis in human life" and they considered death the biggest crisis people had to face. Dr. Ross felt that the best way they could find out about this was to talk to terminally ill patients.

Dr. Ross asked various physicians for permission to talk to patients with terminal disease. "The reactions were varied, from stunned looks of disbelief to rather abrupt changes of topic of conversation; the end result being that I did not get one single chance even to get near such a patient." The physicians, Dr. Ross said, were very defensive when it came to talking about death and dying. They also wished to protect their patients from what they believed would be a shocking experience.

With perserverance, Dr. Ross was finally able to see a patient. He welcomed her with open arms, invited her to sit down, and indicated he was ready to talk. She stopped him at that point, explaining that she would return the next day with her theology students. Dr. Ross admits she was not sensitive enough to understand what the patient was trying to communicate to her. "Little did I realize then that when such a patient says 'Please sit down *now*,' tomorrow may be too late."

When she came back the following day with her students, the patient was too weak to speak and died within an hour.

Since then, Dr. Ross has interviewed more than five hundred dying or terminally ill people. She discovered that most patients *wanted* to talk about themselves and their condition. Surveys have shown that whereas 80 or 90 percent of doctors did not want to tell their patients of the serious nature of their illness, about the same percentage of patients did want to be told. Dr. Ross strongly recommends that the physician tell the patient—but in such a way that hope is not ruled out. Never discuss it in terms of remaining months, she says, but rather in terms of a battle that patient, family, and doctor are going to fight together. Her interviews have shown that the most gravely ill patient keeps open the possibility of continued existence.

These interviews evolved into a seminar, an accredited course. The students were medical interns, chaplains, nurses, psychology students, social workers. The teachers were dying patients. Everyone benefited. Talking with one other human being, Dr. Ross has found, can enable a dying person to come to terms with his or her impending death. Dying in isolation can be the most inhuman—or unhuman—part of the whole process.

From her experience, Dr. Ross learned that there are five psychological stages that the dying pass through—pass through, that is, if they can make it all the way. Often the help of a friend or counselor is needed.

The first stage begins with suspicion of or acquaintance with the terminal illness. The first reaction is denial. "No, not me."

Usually, the person can't keep up the fantasy of denial, although some sufferers never progress beyond the first stage. In the second stage, the person admits the reality and becomes angry. The "No, not me" turns into an embittered "Why me?"

This phase eventually yields to a bargaining attitude. If God has not heeded my angry demands, perhaps he will be more disposed to hear my request if I ask nicely. Dr. Ross likens this attitude to a child's reaction when his parents turn down a request. One young woman patient pleaded to be allowed to go to her brother's wedding. If she were allowed to go, she said, she would make no further fuss about taking her pills and other medicine. When she returned to the hospital, she reminded her doctor that she still had one other unmarried brother.

From bargaining, the patient passes into a state of profound depression. This is a mourning for the loss of himself and all the important people and things in his life. If we survivors lose one person in our lives with the death of a friend or family member, one can imagine the grief at the prospect of losing everyone. Many people, unfortunately, die in this state of hopelessness and resignation. They die giving up.

But with perseverance in gaining insight—sometimes this requires the guidance of a psychiatrist or clergyman, but a loving friend can be the catalyst, too—the dying person can achieve a more positive state. No longer anger at his fate, not depression, but acceptance. Dr. Ross tells of the dying woman who held out against all odds for a miracle. At the end, she said she believed the miracle had happened. She no longer was afraid to die. And, having reached a mental readiness for death, she died.

These stages constitute a recognizable pattern of bereavement. In the case of the dying person, the grieving takes place at the prospect of impending death. Close family members go through a similar psychological process. It is not unusual for patients counseled by Dr. Ross to have reached a state of acceptance before their relatives do. The stages are not necessarily synchronized. The bereavement of survivors after death, where there has been no preparation, may follow a similar pattern, although there is no chance for the bargaining stage.

Psychiatrist Alfred Wiener at Albert Einstein College of Medicine gives these five stages of grief and mourning. At first a person feels numbness when told of the death of a good friend or family member. This numbness helps him to act like a robot, to go through the motions of routine and to arrange a funeral. This is followed by a violent physical reaction, feelings of choking and gasping for breath. This lasts for a brief time, and after it the person comes out of his shock to confront the reality of death. And to grieve. Mourning is marked by a noticeable withdrawal from society. It goes on for three to six months. After that, the person is usually psychologically ready to resume his place in society.

In 1967, the wife of Austin Kutscher died after a long struggle with cancer that was painful to both the wife and the husband. Dr. Kutscher, a professor of dentistry at Columbia University, had so neglected his own health and was so physically vulnerable after his wife's death that he had to be admitted to a hospital for ailments of his own. During this period of bereavement and while in the hospital, medical colleagues sought to console Dr. Kutscher. He and they began to search medical literature for procedures to ease the suffering. They searched and found virtually nothing.

From his personal experience, Dr. Kutscher felt abandoned by the medical profession at a time when he most needed help. Physicians, it seemed, routinely abandoned and took no further responsibility for the bereaved survivors, as though their job ended with the moment of death. In his own experience, Dr. Kutscher found that the abandonment intensified his already abnormal feelings of isolation and loneliness resulting from his wife's death. Bereavement itself is a form of illness, he says. Certainly it predisposes a person to disease. One survey found that a person is 40 percent more likely to die in the year following the death of a husband or wife than other people the same age who do not suffer such a loss.

As a result of his searing experience with death and bereavement, his lack of preparation and competent medical assistance,

Dr. Kutscher went on to help organize in 1968 the Foundation of Thanatology (from *thanatos,* the Greek word for death), an institution to promote medical investigation into the problems of death, bereavement, and grief.

In 1969, Elisabeth Kübler-Ross published her experiences with terminally ill people in what became an enormously popular book, *On Death and Dying.* The following year, Dr. Kutscher, along with psychiatrists Bernard Schoenberg and David Peretz and psychologist Arthur Carr, published *Loss and Grief: Psychological Management in Medical Practice.* This book, called the first textbook in thanatology, also gained wide attention.

A series of books and magazine and newspaper articles began reviving the subject of death, defying the taboo that had ruled for decades. The conspiracy of silence was broken.

Doctors and nurses began attending courses to inform themselves on the subject. Clergymen began to discuss a theology of death, and about a dozen major seminaries began courses on a ministry to the dying. This was necessary because Americans of whatever calling had erected stout psychological defenses against death and needed to be educated on the subject. Some clergymen began to learn in an age of fading belief that a time-tested saying such as "God called him to heaven" might no longer comfort survivors, but instead cause resentment against God.

Calvary Hospital in the borough of the Bronx in New York City instituted what it calls an "integrated approach to death." The medical and nursing staffs, the chaplains and visiting clergymen, and the social service staff work together to meet the physical, spiritual, and psychological needs of the dying. Calvary admits only cancer patients who are poor. Usually their life expectancy is only three to six weeks. Yet 15 percent of the patients admitted to the hospital each year are discharged. Not that they are free of cancer, but that people who find they have something to live for often do so for a while longer.

Other groups want to found institutions patterned after the famous St. Christopher's Hospice in London, where the terminally ill end their existence with first-class treatment. Alcohol and heroin are used if necessary to ease the suffering caused by severely painful illnesses.

Courses on death education have now appeared in hundreds of colleges and high schools. One community college in upstate New York offered a course called "The Psychology of Grief and Dying" to . . . funeral directors.

There is a long way to go to change the American attitude toward dying and death. The defenses are deep and wide and high. The defenders are well entrenched.

But change has begun.

SIX

A Good Death

On April 19, 1957, Hugh Smith and his wife, Lucy, were involved in an auto accident. Smith was found dead at the scene of the accident. Lucy Smith, unconscious, was taken to a hospital. For seventeen days she remained in a coma as a result of brain injury and then died. She never regained consciousness.

The timing of Lucy Smith's death was a matter of great importance to potential heirs. If she survived her husband, then the entire estate was hers before she died, and at her death the claims of her relatives gained precedence. If Mr. and Mrs. Smith died at the same time, then his kin had equal claim to the joint estate.

The Arkansas Supreme Court was asked to rule that Lucy Smith had died at the same time as her husband, since she lost consciousness and power of will at the same moment he did. This was a novel claim at that time because traditionally a person was declared legally dead when he stopped breathing and his heart stopped beating. The Arkansas Supreme Court upheld this tradition. The judge wrote that "it would be too much of a strain of credulity for us to believe any evidence offered to the effect that Mrs. Smith was dead, scientific or otherwise. . . . Likewise, we take judicial notice that one breathing, though unconscious, is not dead."

In 1968, a group of scientists at Harvard Medical School set out

to eliminate the confusion and conflicts over when death has occurred by establishing one definition that would be accepted everywhere. These scientists pointed out that the stopping of breath and
heartbeat had served well enough in the past as the boundary between life and death because it led inevitably to brain death and
to biological death. With today's medical equipment and techniques, however, this first-stage clinical death sometimes could be
reversed and the person restored to life or, what happens more
frequently, breathing and circulation can be revived artificially
even after the brain has died.

These scientists pointed out that once the brain has died there is
no hope for that person to regain conscious, meaningful life. And
so they argued that everyone should agree that when the brain
dies, death has occurred. The scientists showed several ways to
confirm brain death. One way is to turn off the respirator for three
minutes to see whether the person resumes breathing on his own.
Another is to monitor for any electrical activity in the brain. Since
a few unusual conditions can temporarily suppress voluntary
breathing and electrical activity in the brain, the Harvard scientists recommended keeping the unconscious patient on the respirator for twenty-four hours and then retesting. If there are still
no signs of electrical activity or voluntary breathing, then brain
death is certain. The person should and could be declared dead,
they said. Some medical scientists now say there is no reason to
wait so long. If the telltale signs of brain life do not return within
thirty minutes or an hour, the person is beyond restoration to
meaningful life.

There was an urgent and practical reason for declaring a person
dead at this point because of a medical breakthrough since the
ruling of the Arkansas judge.

A trial in Oakland, California, in May 1974, dramatizes what
has happened. The previous September, Andrew Lyons and
Samuel Allen, Jr., had argued at Lyons' house. Tempers flared,

and Lyons pulled a gun and shot Allen in the head. Allen was pronounced dead and Lyons was arrested and charged with homicide. Since Allen's body except for the brain was undamaged, physicians at Highland Hospital kept the rest of the body alive with artificial respiration until they removed the heart and transplanted it in another person.

Lyons then brought a lawsuit charging that Allen had been killed by the doctors who removed his heart, not by the bullet in the brain, because he was still breathing after the injury. To complicate matters, the State of California did not have a legal definition of death. The state accepted the attending physician's decision in each instance. Now Lyons was challenging the medical declaration in the case of Allen. At the trial, a number of expert witnesses testified that the best definition of death is the irreversible halt of brain activity. Nathan Shumway, one of the most successful of all heart transplant specialists, said that the brain is the one determinant of life "because the brain is the one organ that can't be transplanted."

After hearing arguments, the judge instructed the jury that the victim must be considered legally dead from the brain damage inflicted by the bullet. Lyons was found guilty of manslaughter, although his attorney said he would appeal because the judge's instructions did not follow the long-standing legal tradition of death.

This was a case where brain death was complete, so that the person could not go on breathing without artificial help. But what about a case where the brain damage is only partial so that a person lies in a coma but can still breathe and still has normal heartbeat to pump the blood through his body? This person is alive by anybody's definition, although he may still need help to sustain his life. He might have to be fed intravenously. He might need tubes to convey wastes out of his body. But such artificial aids are common for patients in a hospital recovering from intestinal surgery and for many other kinds of ailments. The patients use such aids temporarily, then go home when they are cured.

Such treatment was also given to people in irreversible coma, particularly during the 1950s and 1960s, when the medical means for prolonging life had been powerfully improved but medical experts were vague on the cut-off point for meaningful life. Until everyone was sure that there was no coming back from irreversible brain damage, then doctors and family members could hope for recovery—and in the meantime continue extraordinary measures to preserve that chance. One man in California was kept alive unconscious for eight years with a tube in his bladder; every eight hours a nurse put another tube down his throat to feed him. Special nurses had to attend him around the clock. The cost was $200,000.

These advanced techniques also began prolonging the lives of people so sick with cancer and other sometimes painful conditions that some of them pleaded to be released from their misery. Life was preserved in senile people who didn't know who or where they were, in people paralyzed and mute from stroke, in people so weak from terminal disease they could hardly flutter their eyelids.

A strong reaction developed among a growing number of survivors forced to witness some new kind of ghastly ritual. They had to watch a mother, a husband, a beloved friend tormented by misery that nature would have ended but medical science prolonged. They had to share the humiliation of a parent, a lifelong guide and model, who could no longer feed himself or control his bowels; whose personality was transformed from Jekyll to Hyde by a tumor squeezing his brain. Not to mention the father or wife who was just a breathing vegetable. The witnesses began to wonder whether medicine was prolonging the living . . . or the dying. They began to question if human beings were entitled to less than the merciful death we accord to wounded animals in their agony.

But.

This humane response pointed to a touchy area in human affairs. It meant doing something that adversely affected the patient's chances for survival. It came to be known as "pulling the plug," deliberately cutting off all the remarkable life-support equipment that medical science had developed for the most admirable purpose, saving life. It could mean more than that. It could mean providing the means for the pain-racked person to shorten his life. It could mean helping the person to end his life. It could mean responding to his pleas by taking his life.

The response indicated, in other words, going against one of the strongest prohibitions of human society: "Thou shalt not kill." The moral, religious, and legal prohibitions against homicide have been so strong because, unlike almost all other species of animals, we kill our own kind. Murder goes back to Cain and Abel at the beginning of our species, and we have still not been able to control this impulse in all our members. And so any move to weaken the restraints against taking a human life is met with suspicion. For physicians, the dilemma is worse, because their purpose is to save lives, not to shorten them.

Society's restraints were evident in the highly publicized case of Karen Anne Quinlan. Her fate was debated at a trial in Morristown, New Jersey, in the fall of 1975. The twenty-one-year-old woman had lain in a coma for seven months. She had suffered massive brain damage when her breathing stopped for a period of minutes presumably after taking a combination of tranquilizers and alcohol.

Karen's brain still showed some signs of life, but she required extraordinary medical procedures to keep her living. Her parents, devout Catholics, with the blessing of their priest, asked doctors to turn off the respirator. The parents said they wanted their daughter's future placed in God's hands. The physicians refused the request, and the parents sought legal permission to stop the extraordinary measures.

Five different interests were represented at the trial. Attorneys presented the cases for the parents, for Karen, for the attending physicians, for the hospital, and for the state. At the end of the trial, Judge Robert Muir, Jr., refused to authorize removal of the respirator. He said that was a medical decision. "There is a duty to continue the life-assisting apparatus if, within the treating physician's opinion, it should be done." Judge Muir added: "The single most important temporal quality Karen Anne Quinlan has is life. This court will not authorize that life to be taken from her. There is no constitutional right to die."

Almost everyone who discussed the moral, ethical, legal, and medical issues in the Quinlan case agreed that there are no easy answers.

The suggested humane alternative to prolonged suffering of terminal patients is known as euthanasia, itself a controversial word. It is controversial because it has two meanings. The word itself is from the Greek, meaning an easy death or a good death. That is its original meaning. But it has also come to mean mercy killing—according a merciful death to an individual in misery or pain. The trouble is that in practice euthanasia, mercy killing, has been abused. For instance, Nazi Germany put to death mental patients, retarded people, and others whom the authorities considered incompetent. A precedent was set in ancient Greece by another militaristic state, Sparta. By law, a Spartan father had to submit each child to a state council. If the child appeared normal and strong, he was given an allotment of land. But if the child was judged to be physically or mentally weak, he was thrown off a cliff.

The folly of this policy, not to mention its inhumanity, may be appreciated when you consider that a genius like Einstein didn't speak until he was three years old.

While everyone can agree that these state executions are wrong, the questions can become much more difficult. Was a parent right to take the life of an infant child hideously deformed by Thalidomide? What do you think of that action? What would be your decision (if you could make it and carry it out) if you were the parent? If you were the child? Is life under any circumstances better than nonlife?

In an attempt to deal with such questions, many authorities and experts have reached a broad basis for agreement: Let the dying person have as much control over his fate as possible within the rules of our society.

The New York State Medical Society has stated this policy: "The use of euthanasia is not in the province of the physician. The right to die with dignity, or the cessation of the employment of extraordinary means to prolong the life of the body when there is irrefutable evidence that biological death is inevitable, is the decision of the patient and/or the immediate family with the approval of the family physician." The American Hospital Association has proclaimed a "Bill of Rights for Patients," which includes the right "to refuse treatment to the extent permitted by law" as well as the right to be told exactly what his condition is. And the American Civil Liberties Union has issued a handbook entitled The Rights of Hospital Patients.

A good death to the ancient Greeks meant an easy death free from pain surrounded by fortunate circumstances. To people in medieval times, the good death came to the person in control of his destiny who had enough warning to prepare himself for the next world. In the 1400s and 1500s, the good death was experienced by those devout people who had the strength to resist the last worldly temptation and to reaffirm their faith in God and heaven. And through all ages until our own, human beings could be comforted in their final crisis by dying among those who cared for them.

A variety of circumstances have conspired to rob us of the good death. But mainly they come down to matters of faith. Loss of faith for some people took away the certainty of heaven. We exchanged belief in natural miracles for faith in medical miracles and witnessed so many of these that we refused to accept the inevitability of death in any specific instance. Thus it became difficult to accept death in principle. In some cases, the price paid for extra life was loss of an easy death. Because of our faith in medical science and its promise of salvation, we were willing to give up control of our lives and destinies and risk dying in the isolation of a hospital room.

Now we see attempts to return to the ideal of the good death. There are moves to restore to the person some control over his or her destiny both in the manner and the setting of the final days of life. The person's wishes for an easy death are gaining respect. And he or she is receiving counsel on accepting death. These measures are to be applauded.

But the matter of a good death cannot be left here because it is not that simple. To begin with, life can be more unpredictable than the most astonishing novel. With wars, earthquakes, new inventions, financial booms and recessions, and all the peculiar things that human beings do, it is impossible to know what the circumstances will be at the end of your life. There is no way to guarantee that you will be able to control all the circumstances of your death.

The soldier who throws himself upon a live grenade, sacrificing himself to save the lives of his buddies, has no chance to prepare for his death. One selfless impulse and his life is gone. Many human beings have made similar, instantaneous choices: losing their lives in an attempt to save someone else from drowning or from a fire or from the path of an oncoming automobile.

Similarly, an easy death may not be the death of your choice under the circumstances. Some people have endured the most devilish torture rather than betray their comrades or country. Some people prefer to die without mind-fogging drugs because they wish to experience their final moments with clarity. Jesus died in agony. He could have avoided crucifixion, but in order to do so he would have had to renounce what he stood for, would have had to cancel the life he had lived. In his case, the price of an easy death would have been the negation of his life.

Your death is not an isolated event. It is the last act of your life. The person who dies amidst friends, respected by his community, truly mourned by his fellows has arrived at that position by earning it over a lifetime. A good death cannot be guaranteed, but it is prepared for by living a good life. You are more likely to die with dignity if you have learned to lived with dignity.

And while we are about it, one further word about the subject of acceptance. It is a mark of sanity to accept the inevitability of your death, but be cautious about translating acceptance into submissiveness. Much of the dignity of human existence has come from the struggle against death. And some psychotherapists have discovered that it is easier for some people to die by resisting rather than surrendering to death. In the words of the poet Dylan Thomas: "Do not go gentle into that good night."

If advice seems to conflict, the story of Alexander the Great may help clear up some of the confusion.

In 334 B.C., when Alexander was twenty-two years old and king of Macedon in Greece, he set out with thirty-five thousand men to invade the Persian Empire and free Greek cities along the Asian coast of the eastern Mediterranean Sea from Persian domination. His forces defeated the Persian horsemen in their first battle, although reckless Alexander nearly lost his life in the fighting. This victory freed some of the Greek ports on the Mediterranean, and the Macedonians turned inland. At Gordium, Alexander was shown the famous Gordian knot which, according to legend, Gordius had tied upon his accession as king of the Phrygians. An oracle had declared that whoever undid the Gordian knot would become master of Asia, but the knot was so intricate that for centuries no one was able to untie it. Legend has it that Alexander unsheathed his sword and cut the knot. But historian Harold Lamb says that Alexander untied the knot by pulling out a peg that hid a loose end of the knot.

At Gordium, perhaps influenced by the prophecy, the young general-king disregarded the advice of his older officers and started a drive to the south to capture the Mediterranean bases of the great Persian fleet. On a narrow coastal road, Alexander's expedition was cut off by the Great King Darius III and a veteran army. While the Macedonian infantry and heavy cavalry engaged the enemy head on in a narrow valley, Alexander worked his offensive unit of horsemen across a mountain slope on the right to attack behind the Persian lines. Darius broke and fled in his chariot. With the flight of their leader, the Persian troops lost heart. The first-line army was beaten so badly it was never assembled again.

Alexander went on to conquer the Persian fleet's bases as well as Egypt, where he was proclaimed pharaoh. Now he began to dream of forging his own empire. He founded the city of Alexandria at the mouth of the Nile River, and turned once again toward the Persian forces still commanded by Darius.

This new scheme was not hailed enthusiastically by many Macedonian warriors, who had been away from home for nearly three years. Besides, Darius had offered an attractive peace treaty. He would allow the Macedonians to control all of what is now the Middle East to the Euphrates River and would pay a handsome tribute in gold as well. Alexander's marshal, Parmenion, is reputed to have said that he would accept Darius' offer if he were Alexander. And Alexander replied: "And so would I if I were Parmenion."

Alexander began to march to the east, one of the most remarkable adventures in human history. The farther he went, the longer stretched his supply lines. As fresh units arrived from Macedon, war-weary soldiers were sent home. He crossed the Euphrates, crossed the Tigris River, and then with his force partially made up of untested recruits, clashed with a huge army conscripted from the Persian Empire. Alexander was victorious once again.

Alexander pursued Darius, and finally, with only five hundred Macedonians keeping pace with him, tracked the fugitive across a desert toward the Caspian Sea. He came upon the body of Darius. The Great King had been assassinated by angry and fearful subordinates.

Now the king of Macedon, generalissimo of the Greek armies, pharaoh of Egypt was also Great King of Asia. Surely he was satisfied now. Surely he would turn back. He pressed eastward. And all the while he was building his empire, founding sixty Alexandrias, seeing to the intermarriage of his Greek officers and men with local women along the path of conquest.

Alexander pushed into the hard mountainous country of what is now Afghanistan. He was beyond the world known to the Greeks. The adventure had now become the conquest of the unknown. This decision to go on was too much for some Macedonian officers. They conspired to kill Alexander. He put down the conspiracy and continued eastward.

In Afghanistan, he heard of the river Indus, and drove his expeditionary force across the Hindu Kush mountains. At the Indus River, the Macedonians were an incredible three thousand miles from home! Alexander believed they had entered the last peninsula of the earth. His dream, his consuming purpose, his obsession was now to reach the Ocean of the East. It would be eighteen centuries before Columbus would venture on another such voyage into the unknown.

Alexander crossed the Indus. But at the next river, the Jhelum, the Greeks met hostile forces mounted on armored elephants. The horses were terrified by the strange, huge animals, so the vaunted Macedonian cavalry was useless. Alexander won the battle, nevertheless, with his infantry.

Shaken by this experience, fearful at their fantastic distance from their world, his veteran soldiers mutinied. His own men forced Alexander to do what no others could—to turn back. It was a bitter retreat, for he believed he had almost reached his goal, the end of land. He knew he could never mount such an undertaking again. His dream was over.

In the Indus Valley on the way back, Alexander summoned some philosophers of the Jain sect. The Westerner challenged the wisdom of the East. Alexander's questions reveal what preoccupied his thoughts.

He asked one Jain how a man can become a god.

The Jain replied: "By doing what is impossible for a man to do."

He asked another sage which are more numerous, the living or the dead. The Jain answered that the living are more numerous because the dead no longer exist.

Then Alexander asked: "How long is it good for a man to live?"

A third Jain answered: "As long as he does not prefer death to life."

Alexander never made it back to his native land. Exhausted by carousing and the rigors of the expedition, the adventure ended, the invincible conqueror caught a fever and died in Babylon. He was thirty-two years old.

There is a time for every thing under heaven, says the preacher in Ecclesiastes. "A time to be born, and a time to die." When the time comes, there will not be any great mystery about when to struggle against death and when to accept it.

It could be said that whatever was vital in Alexander died in India when he had to turn his face to the west, although he lived for another two and a half years. It happens frequently that people's lives are concluded before they die. Death is an afterthought, a postscript, P.S.

And who can say this is not a good way to go?

 SEVEN

Coping with Death

We have seen that the attempt to deny death not only is futile but cuts us off from reality. It cripples our ability to deal with death. Denial is an ineffective defense against death.

Not only must we acknowledge death, but recognize it for what it is. The death of a person we care about deeply is not just another natural occurrence. It is a profound, wounding experience.

Here is an account of its impact by a man who wrote to the *New York Times* nearly two years after his wife's death:

> Arranging for her funeral while she lay in a coma with death imminent was an activity I find hard to believe I went through. It was the last thing in the world I had ever wanted to do, but it had to be done, although I was still too dazed to fully comprehend the impact of losing the person in the world I loved most dearly.
>
> We had shared so many years together, we had shared so many wonderful and exciting experiences, we were so much in love and such inseparable companions, the very idea that one of us would die and leave the other alone and bereaved seemed so remotely distant that we refused to entertain it and spoil our fun. . . .
>
> I miss her terribly and I have agonized—nearly to the point of self-destruction.
>
> I am living a loneliness I never expected. I feel so vulnerable, so inferior, so unsure of myself.
>
> I find no purpose in living, though I have been told that purpose

will eventually manifest itself. There are no fond expectations, no stimulating goals, no promising future.

Everything seems different—even the newspaper she loved so much and the news magazine that could disturb her routine if it arrived a day late. We frequented so many places I am constantly reminded of her; the music we shared I cannot bear to hear now. What anguish to come home night after night to an apartment devoid of her warmth and radiance.

Death has meaning only for us, the living. If it has significance for the dead, we do not know about it. Our deepest attitudes on the subject are formed by what we have learned of other people dying. We have seen the agony of dying, the tragedy of death, the unexpectedness of it portrayed on television, in the movies, in newspapers, in magazines and books, and in person. Contemplating death, we react with one predominant emotion.

"They wanted to give me the last sacraments," his mother-in-law tells Dr. Zhivago from her sickbed in Boris Pasternak's famous novel. "Death is hanging over me. . . . It may come any moment. . . . When you go to have a tooth out you're frightened, it'll hurt, you prepare yourself. . . . But this isn't a tooth, it's everything, the whole of you, your whole life . . . being pulled out. . . . And what is it? Nobody knows. . . . And I am sick at heart and terrified."

This fear of death is embedded in the depths of our nature. A psychologist who investigated primitive myths, Joseph Henderson, says the fear of death goes back to some primal pattern in human experience, a pattern that we can no longer recall. Anthropologist Bronislaw Malinowski thought that the fear might go even farther back into the mists of our past. He found that primitive people were intensely afraid of death "probably as the result of some deep-seated instinct common to animals and man."

One is tempted, with this in mind, to concede that the fear of death is beyond our control.

As it happens, fear and control are closely related. Our primitive forebears feared thunder and echoes and dozens of natural happenings that do not hold us in awe today. They were petrified by the voodoo curse that has no effect on us. Why?

In 1972, about nineteen thousand Americans were victims of homicide. That same year, three times that number of Americans were killed in automobile accidents. Yet Americans fear muggers and feel safe in the family car; they are far more preoccupied with police security than they are with highway safety. People who double-bolt their doors and are afraid to walk the streets at night scoff at fastening seat belts and drive at night after drinking liquor. Why?

The answer is that we become fearful in a situation in which we do not exercise control. There was a time back in our evolutionary past when our earliest ancestors had every right to fear lions and leopards, and the only defense was not to get caught. Muggers, robbers, holdup men are our present-day predators, who happen to be members of our own species. As victims of crimes, we are caught in situations beyond our control.

Primitive people were afraid of thunder and echoes because they believed those phenomena were harmful. Once we understood the nature of these occurrences, we lost or learned to control our fear. Knowledge gave us control and a feeling of safety.

Sailing along in our well-engineered cars at fifty-five miles an hour over well-designed highways, we are rarely aware of the potential violence stored in the high speed until we suddenly stop or change direction. Sitting inside the car's shell, we feel protected. With the car under our conscious direction, we feel that the situation is in control. We are not afraid because we *think* we are safe.

Where else can we feel more secure than in our own home surrounded by familiar things and persons? Yet falls on stairways, accidental stabbings with sharp utensils, electric shocks, wounds from power tools are mass killers. And they arouse no apprehension in any of us.

From this perspective, human history can be seen as the record of one long, continuous effort to achieve control. Early on, the Greek philosopher-scientist Aristotle said that the goal of evolution is mastery of the environment. Control of events and environment was the aim of magic, our primitive form of reasoning. Anthropologist James Frazer believed that when people became more sophisticated and realized that magic didn't work very well, they turned to religion to explain the mysteries of nature. While religion relied upon an unprovable deity, it also revealed deep insights into the human psyche and championed many kinds of social justice.

Finally, according to Frazer, religion was followed by a new system of thought: science. Science was the most successful in enlarging our control. Magic and science are alike in that they make associations of ideas and use deduction. But magic made faulty associations while science insisted upon rigorous proof. Knowledge is power, said Francis Bacon, an English philosopher who lived at the time of Shakespeare and who was the first great champion of science. We can see how right he was. Through science we can build skyscrapers, send men to the moon, see distant galaxies, and transplant a heart from one human being to another.

But one event remains invincible in spite of all our science and knowledge. We cannot control death. We cannot postpone it the way we do a checkup at the dentist, we cannot avoid it as we do the summer heat in our air-conditioned rooms, nor can we eliminate it as we are doing with smallpox. Death is the supreme event in our experience that is beyond our control. Moreover, we don't really understand it. We don't know whether something exists beyond death or whether it is the slide into extinction. For these reasons as well as the pain and the loss of dignity sometimes associated with death, we regard this ending of our lives with all the emotions clustered about fear.

What we see here are two different sets of attitudes toward death. At the death of a person close to us, we feel bereavement, grief, sorrow. When we think of death-to-be, particularly our own deaths or those of people we love, then the emotion is likely to be apprehension, anxiety, fear.

Let us turn to the first of these circumstances: dealing with the death of someone we love. The primary fact is that the survivor has lost someone precious. He is bereaved, he experiences an acute sense of loss.

Now, we are inflicted with loss in various ways all through life. Often we are hardly conscious of these lesser bereavements, and we adjust naturally to these stresses with little conscious thought. Children particularly have a high quotient of adaptability, so much so that the loss of this resilience is often given as a primary characteristic of aging. Families that move to new communities as the father changes jobs must accommodate to losses of friends and associations. Even for the children in stay-put families, there is perpetual change and loss in growing up. Beginning school interferes with the close relationship with mother. Each year, you take new subjects and face more difficult challenges at school. Every four years or so, you change schools. With each year, your body has changed and so has your outlook on life. Even the disappearance of a candy store that was a landmark in your neighborhood and a favorite haunt in your childhood can exert its effect. If enough of the old houses are replaced by new apartment buildings, if enough of the old neighbors move away to be replaced by strangers, one's sense of community disintegrates. A person has a choice of living with memories—living in the past—or adjusting to the future that is coming.

Death is the ultimate bereavement. And the death of a husband or wife is the severest blow we can take. This was the finding of psychiatrist Thomas Holmes and his colleagues at the University of Washington School of Medicine, based on twenty years of research. Dr. Holmes and Captain Richard Rahe of the Naval Health Research Center in San Diego set up a scale to rate the intensity of stresses we face in life. It is a list of forty-three of the most common stressful events in our society. At the top of the list is the death of a wife or husband, to which the scientists assigned a value of 100. Next in order come divorce, marital separation, jail term, and, in fifth place, death of a close family member. Divorce has a stress impact of 73, death of a close family member a value of 63. Death of a close friend is rated at 37. Other typical situations causing stress are ending school, change to a different line of work, loss of job.

By quantifying these stresses, one gets a better idea of how severe they are. If too many stresses pile up at one time, we are likely to get sick, physically or mentally. For instance, if a father dies (death of a close family member: 63 points), greatly curtailing the family income (change in financial state: 38), forcing the family to move to another neighborhood (change in residence: 20), forcing you to leave school (ending school: 26) and go to work (change to different line of work: 36), changing your social activities (18) and recreation (19)—there is a good chance you will get sick. That is a total of 220 stress points. In one test of the scale, Dr. Holmes found that an average of seventeen of twenty people who scored above 300 points in a year suffered a change in health. Of those with 150 points or more, about half experienced a health change.

As you can see, most of the stresses are associated with loss, bereavement. We respond to bereavement with grief. At the death of a beloved person, grief is an intense and painful emotion. And a complex one. Its main component is sadness or the longer-lasting sorrow. But there can be anguish, remorse, guilt, shame, anger, fear, apprehension. The constellation of emotions at such a death can encompass yearning, dejection, depression, nervousness, agitation, panic, despair, hopelessness, helplessness, shock, denial, numbness, relief, emptiness.

A psychiatrist who has studied this subject, David Peretz,

learned that the makeup of a person's grief is conditioned by his relationship to the dead person during life. We tend to regard mother, father, brother, sister, and others important to us as models. They are needed, loved, envied, idealized, and sometimes hated. By imitating and identifying with these models, a child learns how to deal with the anxieties and problems of living.

At the death of one of these "model" persons, the grief will consist mainly of sadness and sorrow if the main ingredient in the association were idealization. But when the relationship was marked by hostility or fear, then guilt and anxiety will make their appearance in the grieving. Few human relationships are perfect. Many or most are characterized by a certain amount of ambivalence—occasional swings to annoyance, anger, or hatred as well as love—so that feelings of guilt and anxiety are mixed in with grief. This is normal. Nothing to be ashamed of. Feelings of guilt may be expressed by over-idealizing the dead person. "If I had only known. . . ." "If I had it to do over again. . . ."

Most physicians who were asked about it observed that guilt was less likely when there had been a free expression of feelings before the death. In other words, concealing from a person that he has cancer or some fatal disease—for the most worthy reasons—can carry its own burden of postmortem guilt.

Other unexpected emotions may erupt. Anger, for instance. A resentment that the person has died, taking with him his comforting love and support.

The bereaved person must cope with these hard-to-deal-with emotions in addition to the essential grief. One often used mechanism for dealing particularly with anxiety is repression. Then we see the dry-eyed mourner who shows no grief or any other emotions. Or there is the person who vents great hostility upon the supposed failures of the physicians and hospital. Or the person who goes haywire, becoming sexually promiscuous or turning into a frantic alcoholic. These are unhealthy responses to bereavement, for they avoid confronting the loss and integrating it in the self. There is no resolution. The psychic wound never heals, or never heals properly.

Bereavement is like an illness. Experiencing grief, expressing grief is nature's way of healing us. Tears, crying, wailing, loss of appetite, clenched fists, grimacing, pacing back and forth are the painful first steps toward the restoration of health. They evoke gestures of solace from friends and relatives, helpful and important elements in the process. The positive aspect of grief and mourning can be likened to a period of convalescence during which the emotional ties to the dead person can be gradually withdrawn so that the person's energies can be reassembled for new transactions with life.

Long before the discipline of psychiatry, Ralph Waldo Emerson, who had experienced the loss of many dear ones in his life, expressed it this way in his essay, "Compensation":

> The death of a dear friend, wife, brother, lover, which seemed nothing but privation, somewhat later assumes the aspect of a guide or genius; for it commonly operates revolutions in our way of life, terminates an epoch of infancy or of youth which was waiting to be closed, breaks up a wonted occupation, or a household, or style of living, and allows the formation of new ones more friendly to the growth of character. It permits or constrains the formation of new acquaintances and the reception of new influences that prove of the first importance to the next years; and the man or woman who would have remained a sunny garden-flower, with no room for its roots and too much sunshine for its head, by the falling of the walls and the neglect of the gardener is made the banyan of the forest, yielding shade and fruit to wide neighborhoods of men.

There are certain aids that can help us deal with the crisis of a beloved person's death. First of all, preparation can start with earliest childhood. At age two and three, the child can be acquainted with the concepts of living and nonliving. With dead flies, mosquitoes, birds, and animals, the subject of death can be introduced in the context of its naturalness. If the subject is treated calmly, matter-of-factly, then the child processes this information with all the other facts he is receiving. Scrupulously avoiding the subject of death in front of a child is not protecting him from a harsh fact of life, but depriving him of the preparation necessary to cope with one of the most difficult of human crises. He is like a person who has never been taught to swim who nevertheless must jump into the water when the boat springs a leak.

Above all, parents should be honest in explaining human death. Not only is it inaccurate to explain that "grandpa has gone to sleep," but a child is likely to accept this explanation literally—and become afraid to go to sleep for fear of dying.

Children should be allowed to attend a funeral with the rest of the family. For better or worse, the death of a close family member is a significant event in their living. They cannot be shielded successfully from it nor is it wise that they should be. If a child is reluctant to attend the funeral service, one should explain what is entailed and let him make up his own mind. If then he prefers not to attend, his decision should be accepted.

Death ceremonies serve valuable psychological and social purposes. Ostensibly, they are held as a tribute to the person who has died, but actually they provide valuable benefits for the living. Since far back in prehistory, funeral rituals have helped human beings weather the shock and pain of an emotional amputation. It is a traditionally tested way to help the survivors adjust to a new reality. At the same time, the custom permits friends and neighbors of the family to reaffirm the bonds of the living.

The displaying and viewing of the corpse in the funeral home has been criticized as a morbid procedure. But there is a certain value in seeing the body of the deceased. It helps the mourners accept the reality of his death. Dr. Elisabeth Kübler-Ross says this witnessing is especially important in cases where the person was a victim of suicide or an automobile accident and was horribly mutilated. There is a tendency in such cases for the hospital to prevent the family from seeing the remains. "It is important that the nurses prepare the body in an acceptable fashion so that the family can view at least part of an identifiable body in order to face the reality of the death," she says.

A question Dr. Ross has been asked is: "When a patient has just died, the relatives are asked to come into the room. Some of them actually talk to the deceased, touch him or even kiss him. Don't you think this is morbid?" Dr. Ross answers: "No, I don't think this is morbid. I am much more concerned about people who appear very stoic, calm, detached, and outwardly very composed; those who do not say a word or shed a tear; those who are afraid to even look at the body and quietly leave the room. They will eventually have a delayed reaction which may be worse."

When a family has spent three days, as is the Christian practice, or seven days, the traditional Jewish practice, in the formal mourning ritual, the reality of death is imprinted upon the members' minds and emotions. At the same time, they have used an accepted social structure allowing them to express grief. This is becoming almost a luxury in a society that reacts with distaste to private emotional outbursts and applauds tightly controlled behavior.

In the American setting, funeral rituals have been weakened and secularized—that is, shifted from the church to the funeral home. The wake, an all-night vigil for the dead person, was an important feature of Roman Catholic death rites that gave a good opportunity for mourners to express their feelings. It is being abandoned. In most Protestant mourning ceremonies, the funeral service is conducted at the funeral home. The de-ritualizing of the mourning procedure tends to make it more difficult for survivors to cope with their grief. They are cut adrift from traditional avenues of expression and must work through this trying period more on their own.

With a funeral home handling details, an important and practical commercial aspect enters into the death ceremonies. An average funeral in the United States today costs between $1,600 and $2,000. Each item desired—another limousine, a flower car, *In Memoriam* cards—adds to the bill. But by far the most expensive item is the casket. Funeral directors have been criticized for displaying caskets in such a way as to lead or pressure people into buying more expensive caskets than they want or need. Then, too, that latent guilt that is so common and normal in grief spurs mourners to demonstrate their love through the purchase of an unnecessarily costly casket.

Obviously, people suffering from shock and grief are in a poor frame of mind to conduct a business transaction. Again, the best protection is preparation. As distasteful as it may be, one should inquire beforehand at a mortuary when the mind and emotions are not befogged by bereavement. It is also useful to know that there are memorial societies, groups that will conduct funerals and burials very simply but with dignity at low cost.

On the other hand, it is important to many people—many poor people—to be assured that they will have an elegant funeral and burial at the end of their hard lives. Many poor people enter into arrangements whereby they pay a dollar or two a week for most of their lives in order to provide for this satisfactory end.

There is something reassuring to many of us about a sturdy casket or entombment in a marble crypt. It suggests that the beloved dead person will go on in perpetuity, undisturbed. The indestructibility of the cocoon conveys a kind of victory over death. But we should recognize this as part of our irrational heritage. The corpse is putrefying just as surely, if more slowly, inside its impregnable capsule as it would in a pine coffin. The only difference is that entombment imprisons the elements, preventing them from re-entering the ecological pool from which they can help form new life.

As we have learned, burial is an—perhaps *the*—identifying custom of our species. But another prehistoric method of disposal of the body is cremation. Cremation was generally practiced among the upper social classes in ancient Greece and Rome, but fell into disrepute in the Judaeo-Christian world. Ancient Judaism practiced earth burial. There is no biblical prohibition against cremation, but it was used only to dispose of large numbers of bodies after battles or catastrophe. Roman authorities often cremated the bodies of Christian martyrs as a way of preventing their resurrection from the dead, as the Christians believed. In this way, cremation became associated with paganism and was ignored in the Western world for some fifteen centuries.

During the past century, cremation has been resumed in the Western world. It seems to be a preferred means of disposal where population pressures are high. About three of every four people who die in Japan are cremated; more than half the people in England; and high percentages in Sweden, Denmark, and Switzerland. In the United States, the figure is less than 5 percent, with most of the cremations taking place in California, Florida, and the metropolitan areas. The cost of cremation can be about the same as burial, cheap or expensive, depending upon the type of funeral desired.

Two other practical matters. Every person who is the head of a family or the owner of property should have a will. If a person dies intestate—without a will—then his property is divided according to the laws of the state, and that distribution may be contrary to the person's wishes. Furthermore, the state appoints an executor, or administrator, of the will. The appointee must be paid a fee that is taken from the estate. With a will, a person picks as an executor some person close to him whom he can trust to carry out his wishes faithfully.

A certain amount of insurance—enough to defray funeral expenses, at the least—is another virtual necessity to ease the crisis of death for the bereaved.

Finally, the time of death is an opportunity for us to show our humanity. As a friend or neighbor or distant relative of the bereaved, the period of mourning is the time to show that you care.

By a visit to the funeral home, a visit to the home, a note of sympathy, a gift of flowers or some other memorial token, you can share the burden and help lift it slightly.

Now let us turn to ways people have tried to cope with death in the abstract, so to speak—the concept of inevitable death and specifically our own death to come.

The most obvious method in our experience is the denial, through such religions as Christianity, Muhammadanism and Hinduism, that the person's spirit perishes with his physical body. The flesh is mortal, the spirit immortal. Hindus believe in the transmigration of souls, as we mentioned in Chapter Two: after death, the spirit inhabits a new life form in what is known as reincarnation. The Christian-Muslim belief is that there will be a resurrection of bodies and souls at some future time for consignment to an everlasting heaven or hell. Judaism has embraced resurrection to some extent, but it does not play as great a role in the Jewish religion. The Christian belief in resurrection has become intermixed with the Platonic belief in immortal souls that continue to exist after the death of the body.

Now, belief in a spiritual afterlife has been a comfort, a bulwark for countless human beings. It has helped people to meet death and to accept it. Indeed, because of the belief, some people looked forward to release from this imperfect world in exchange for a better one. The erosion of religious faith in our times has had the effect of weakening this defense against death for some contemporary people. Unable to rely on this comforting belief, they must find other means of coping with this basic dread.

Interestingly, some philosophies have dealt with death by reversing the strategy: maintaining that death is the end of everything, annihilation. Lucretius, a Roman philosopher-poet who lived in the first century B.C., made it his goal to rid the human mind of the fear of death. Lucretius was a champion of Epicureanism. Among other things, Epicureans believed that everything is composed of atoms and after death there is only dissolution back to atoms. So, said Lucretius, why be afraid of death? It is an end to misery, an end to fear, and the dead person is safely beyond the reach of revenge and punishment. This is really a pretty good fate when you stop to think about it, he argued. It could be a lot worse. Therefore: stop worrying!

Lucretius was a sickly man who was intensely unhappy living in the Roman society of his time. Believing as he did, he committed suicide when he was forty-four years old.

Another philosopher, David Hume, who lived in Scotland in the eighteenth century, also believed that death meant annihilation. He won much admiration for the serenity with which he met death at the age of sixty-five. A friend noted in his diary in April 1776, when Hume had been ailing for a year and four months before his death: "Mr. Hume this day told me that he had bought a piece of ground; and when I seemed surprised . . . he said it was in the New Church-Yard, on the Carlton Hill, for a burying place; that he meant to have a small monument erected, not to exceed in expense one hundred pounds. . . . I desired him to change the discourse. He did so, but seemed surprised at my uneasiness."

Dr. Johnson, according to his equally famous biographer James Boswell, simply didn't believe that Hume was being honest. "It is more probable that he lied than that so very improbable a thing should be as a man not be afraid of death; of going into an unknown state and not being uneasy at leaving all that he knew." Boswell himself believed that Hume, the great skeptic, was secretly a Christian.

The fact was that Hume was brought up as a Calvinist. A main belief of this Protestant sect is that a person is predestined to spend eternity either in heaven or hell and that there really is very little he can do about it. As a young man, Hume lived with the fear of hell rather than the hope of heaven. At the age of thirty-seven, he fell gravely ill and went through his own personal hell terrified of impending damnation. When he recovered, he went on to convince himself that immortality after death is an illusion. This freed him from his deepest fears, and when death came twenty-eight years later he was able to meet it with an attitude of peace.

How to achieve this acceptance of death has been a main pursuit of philosophers. Socrates drank poison, as ordered by the authorities in Athens, with great calm in the midst of his friends and followers. Of course, Socrates was betting that his soul was immortal and he could spend his future at what he liked best—thinking.

Henry Thoreau, perhaps America's greatest philosopher and most original thinker, died of tuberculosis at the age of forty-five. He'd had many months to consider his impending death and died with serenity. When one visitor to his bedside inquired whether he had made his peace with God, Thoreau replied, "We have never quarreled." And when another speculated about the hereafter, Thoreau said, "One world at a time."

There is the element of courage present as well as philosophy in the way one meets death. As Shakespeare has Julius Caesar say shortly before his assassination: "Cowards die many times before their deaths; / The valiant never taste of death but once."

The Hindu religion has given us yet another method of coping with death and the fear of death. This is transcendence, the yogi's search for pure being, to liberate himself from self-centeredness in order to merge with Ultimate Reality or the soul of the universe. Buddha taught his disciples to seek nirvana, a state of blessed peace in which all desires are extinguished.

Some believe that for just a moment the artist transcends his earthly condition to touch eternal harmonies, achieving a unity with whatever is universal in existence.

The artist does leave behind his works, and even though he dies, he remains immortal in the minds of people who come afterward. The Roman poet Horace boasted that he had wrought monuments more enduring than the pyramids, which are subject to wind and rain. People have gained a kind of immortality (fame) through other kinds of endeavors: by heroic efforts on battle and athletic fields, through discoveries, inventions, great services to mankind. Some people have buildings named after them or endow scholarships at universities or have their figures cast in bronze.

With modern technology, this preservation of a person can be carried to great lengths. One's image, actions, voice can be recorded faithfully on film and videotape. Science-fiction writer Frederik Pohl envisioned an even more complete electronic immortality. A person's experiences, beliefs, thoughts would be programmed into a computer; his voice and language would be tape-recorded so that any combination of words and sentences could be selected. After the person's death, anyone could still converse with the "dead" man or woman.

The most common form of achieving immortality is through having children. But while the reproduction of the self is apparent in the next immediate generation, the strain is diluted with each succeeding generation—heredity dwindling to one-quarter in grandchildren and one-eighth in great-grandchildren. In a few more generations, the trace of the individual has all but disappeared in the river of humanity.

Some people take encouragement from the thought that the elements making up their bodies today are immortal and in the future will constitute other living things. In that sense, they never die. A growing number of people are bequeathing parts of themselves that can go on living in someone else after the donor's death. So far, there have been more than ten thousand kidney and cornea transplants in the United States, more than five thousand skin transplants, and about two hundred heart transplants.

A few people conquer the fear of death by deliberately risking their lives. These are the daredevils, high-speed racing drivers, soldiers of fortune, thrill seekers. They overcome their fear by challenging death. Of course, a good number of these people live abbreviated lives, a price they are willing to pay for their liberation from the human fear.

Some people try to defeat death. They become physicians and heal people who are sick. Many of these acts are temporary victories over death. Other people become scientists and seek out the cause of yellow fever or malaria. Very occasionally, they achieve major victories, adding years to the lives of millions of people. Through science, we may be able to extend human life spans perhaps double or triple what they are now. But when the goal becomes elimination of death itself, the pursuit begins to depart from reality.

Immortality seems to be very desirable to us. It characterizes what we call heaven—but hell, too. If you stop to think about it, really think about it, our notions of heaven are vague. A place populated by all "good" people who live forever certainly does not resemble anything in our experience. Try to imagine for a minute what the world would be like if everyone were immortal. For one thing, it would get a lot more crowded than it is now unless people stopped having children. No more children? That in itself would make it a far less interesting world, a far less lovable world. In a way, the whole point of our lives is to make sure that life is carried on successfully by the next generation, which is mainly why we have marriages, homes, families, schools. That is the strategy of life: to be reborn continually in new individuals so that our very old world remains perpetually new.

At the breaking up of Camelot, Sir Bedivere asks King Arthur, "Where shall I go? Why should Camelot end?" And Arthur answers, in Tennyson's famous poem:

> The old order changeth, yielding place to new,
> And God fulfills Himself in many ways,
> Lest one good custom should corrupt the world.

We have reasons to believe that nature makes provision for our dying, seeing to it in most cases that it is not a painful experience.

As we saw, the most common cause of death is the lack of oxygen to the brain. Not only is this not painful, but anoxia can be a pleasant experience.

Lewis Thomas, the head of Memorial Sloan-Kettering Cancer Center in New York City, says doctors are learning from the revival of people from clinical death after heart attacks that these people did not suffer from fear or anguish. Several of them were conscious of the frantic medical efforts to revive them even though they appeared to be quite dead. What they recalled of this experience was a sensation of detachment and peacefulness.

Dr. Thomas cites the experience of the African explorer David Livingstone, who was caught by a lion and crushed across the chest by the animal's powerful jaws. Livingstone was saved from death by a lucky shot that killed the lion. Dr. Thomas says Livingstone "was so amazed by the extraordinary sense of peace, calm, and total painlessness associated with being killed that he constructed a theory that all creatures are provided with a protective physiologic mechanism, switched on at the verge of death, carrying them through in a haze of tranquillity." Dr. Thomas said he himself had seen agony in death only once, in a patient with rabies.

Perhaps, just perhaps, there is a vaccine for the emotional pain of dying as well. The Scottish philosopher David Hume, who had managed to overcome the fear of death, took consolation in the thought of having achieved everything he meant to do in life. This consisted of his writings and having provided for the financial security of his friends and relatives.

A plaque in a World War II Australian cemetery at Gona in the Pacific reads:

> Here we lie dead because we did not choose
> To shame the land from which we sprung.
> Life is, perhaps, no great thing to lose
> But young men think it is, and we were young.

That quatrain applies to all young people cut down. Death's sting is to die unfulfilled. A vaccine against this mortal sting is to live a full life, a rewarding life, and, if possible, a long life.

In short, while you have the chance, *live.*

 EIGHT

Your Life and Death

Statistically, death is remote from a young person. The prime of life lies ahead.

So why bother to think about death?

The answer is: Because your death is connected to your life. The way you live will probably determine how you die—even when.

Philosophers have taken time and effort to make it clear that ends and means are united. The end grows out of the means as the flower grows out of the stem.

An example of how this works. Let us suppose we have a political leader in office who has been involved in acts harmful to society. It is desirable and important to remove him from office. Now, there are several ways this can be done. If the person is suspected of some criminal wrongdoing, then he can be brought before a court of law and, if found guilty, sent to jail. Impeachment proceedings can be undertaken, as in the case of President Nixon. At the next election, he could be voted out of office. Or he could be assassinated.

Each of these means achieves the removal of the person from political power. But do we really have the same ends? Three of the methods are legal, one is outside the law. By following any of the first three means, citizens abide by the orderly, lawful processes by which society can right wrongs. The last method flouts the spirit of democracy as well as the letter of the law. It says: to hell with the will of the majority, to hell with the rules, one person or a small group shall decide for all. The office holder is gone in both cases. But in one, the laws have been upheld and strengthened. In the other, he was removed illegally. Lawful acts reinforce the long effort to create and maintain civilization. Law*less* acts lead away from civilization toward anarchy and eventually threaten the welfare of all. So ends that appear to be the same can vary widely, depending on the routes taken.

Father William Frazier of Maryknoll Seminary in Westchester, New York, has a surprising way of showing the life-death connection. This is the way he presented it to a death-education class at Yorktown High School, Yorktown Heights, New York:

First he writes the word "life" on a blackboard. Some distance away he writes the word "death." He draws a long arrow leading from life to death. Then he draws two shorter arrows leading back from death toward life, so that it looks like this:

$$\text{LIFE} \; \text{-----------------} \begin{matrix} \Longleftarrow \text{----} \\ \text{----}\Longrightarrow \\ \Longleftarrow \text{----} \end{matrix} \; \text{DEATH}$$

What if, Father Frazier asks, life and death in some sense are woven together? What if they are circular? If death merges into life in some mysterious way, then all our rigid defenses against death become defenses against life. By denying death, we deny life.

Does that make sense? he asked the class. No response. The twenty high school students were not ready to commit themselves.

The clergyman, who has studied people's attitudes toward death not only in the United States but in South America and other parts of the world, was ready to go on.

Is there any sense in which death asserts itself in freedom and decision-making? Death, as he defined it, is "the closing off of all possibilities." Decisions by their very nature do close off possibilities. For example, you may have many talents. You may excel in playing a musical instrument. You may also be a very good athlete. At the same time, you may have a keen interest in science and would like to help people through medical research. But you also like to deal with people and are good at organization so that you could be a successful administrator.

You cannot select all courses. You can't ride off in four different directions at the same time. You must narrow your choices in order to realize the potentiality of one or at most a few callings to the fullest. It's not only a choice *for* something, but a decision *against,* to exclude areas of life. Making these decisions means a partial dying, cutting down life's potential.

Pulling back from the crowd is like dying. The group goes on, the crowd is immortal; only individuals die. In the play *Rhinoceros* by Eugene Ionesco, people turn into a crowd of rhinoceroses, each following the other because he feels he must conform to the group. All change except for one fellow who chooses to remain himself. But he is lonely.

Some people say marriages are made in heaven. "We know that's not true," says Father Frazier. There are many people we could share our lives with. The problem is not just to select a mate, but to exclude candidates, to relinquish so many interesting possibilities in life. "But unless I dedicate myself to that one person, the love will not bloom." Love is a radical self-giving. The more intense the commitment, the more painful the loss. Commitment means bereavement, means willingness to face up to death.

Some people have such strong defenses against death that they are unwilling to make a full commitment to any person or cause or vocation. They protect themselves by turning away from life, and never live.

Psychologist Robert Jay Lifton puts it this way: "To open oneself to love and growth is to become vulnerable also to loss and disillusionment." He cites several ways in which young people escape facing anxiety without seeming to avoid it. One technique is to become extremely intellectual, exploring new alternatives in thought and conversation, but avoiding actual changes or commitments. Another is to develop an ascetic style. Under the guise of discipline, the person tightly controls his life . . . and avoids risks. A third approach, Dr. Lifton says, is to conform, be like everyone else. "This enables one to feel a sense of connection and shared participation, again without confronting one's own fears and doubts."

It was discussed earlier how people react when they are told they have cancer or some other fatal disease. Commonly, the first reaction is disbelief and denial—"Not me." The second stage is anger, and the question—"Why me?" For the terminal patient, it is usually too late to save his life even if he can find the answers.

It is far more useful to ask that question early in life when something can be done about it.

To begin with, we usually think of longevity—and let's face it, longevity is the best measure we have for the successful adjustment to the circumstances of life—in terms of our genes. If you want to have a long life, the truism goes, pick long-lived parents. Now, there is truth in that statement, but it is not the whole truth. What is misleading and downright harmful about it is the suggestion that the length of our lives is biologically predestined. This encourages the belief that the situation is out of our hands, beyond our control. Kismet—it's fated.

Nothing could be further from the truth.

It is a fact that a person born with a crucial defect will have a shortened life. But what happens most often is that we are born with a *predisposition* to some weakness. If your family has a history of heart attacks and strokes, then you may be more *likely* to get cardiovascular disease. The late President Lyndon Johnson became virtually obsessed by this subject. His father had died at age sixty from a heart attack, and Johnson had already suffered one heart seizure when he had his own and his family's medical history fed into a computer. The computer predicted that he would not live beyond the age of sixty-four. Johnson met the deadline, dying at sixty-four.

However, we are learning that it takes other factors, such as stress and the way we behave, to set a disease in motion. Lyndon Johnson's last years were marked by disillusionment with the outcome of the war in Vietnam. He was deeply troubled by the tremendous division the war caused among the American people. He was burdened by psychological stress. He resumed smoking. He let his weight build up. Did Lyndon Johnson give up?

An extensive study by researchers at Duke University with people sixty years and older in Durham, North Carolina, found almost no similarity between the longevity or predicted longevity of subjects in the study and the life span of their parents. Gerontologist (a scientist who studies aging) Erdman Palmore interprets this discovery to mean that inherited disease and genetic imperfections probably do cause early deaths. But for people who have survived sixty years, hereditary influences are overridden by the effects of sixty years of living.

A mass survey of people eighty years and older in the Soviet Union showed that only between 28 and 40 percent of them had parents who had lived to very old age. Remember—you inherit more than genes from your parents. You also get a set of attitudes, code of beliefs, style of living, and in the first part of your life the same environment in which to live. But this inheritance is not as rigid as genes. Children frequently live quite different lives from their parents and move to different places. The circumstances of life change quickly in our society and with them the chances for survival.

Arnold Hutschnecker, an experienced and wise physician in New York City, suggests that only successful livers die normally. Most people die prematurely. This is true, he says, if we make the reasonable assumption that normal death is death from old age.

> From that point of view death is no struggle, nor is it a state of indecision or fear. Instead, it seems a desired state at a time when life with all its complexities becomes too burdensome to cope with. When a person of advanced age dies, we must keep in mind the lowered resistance resulting from the wear and tear of aging, regardless of the clinical diagnosis we physicians write on the death certificate. If we accept this concept of longevity, then most cases now being classified as "death from natural causes," such as cancer or heart attack, are really not natural but must rather be considered death from unnatural causes.

The most direct cause of premature death is suicide. It is an option that is open to every person and has probably been considered by almost everybody at one time or another. Suicide is a difficult subject to generalize about, its instances are so varied and complex. Yet the Jain's answer to Alexander's question "How long is it good for a man to live?" "As long as he does not prefer death to life," certainly applies with full force.

Whatever the circumstances, whoever the person, the act of suicide testifies to a deep incompatibility with life. In many cases, this profound disharmony between the person and his or her circumstances has been preceded by a series of failures to satisfy needs and cope with the challenges of existence. A growing sense of despair or failure or isolation or inadequacy or loss or depression or hopelessness finally goes beyond control and becomes unbearable. Through suicide, the person reasserts mastery of his fate.

It is interesting that control is closely associated with suicide. Medical authorities say that the terminal cancer patient most likely to commit suicide is the one accustomed to exerting control over himself and others. Some terminal patients have exercised control over their situation as a final act of devotion. They shortened their lives to spare their families extended medical expenses. Suicide can be a defiant fist-shaking at destiny. One thousand Jews who were besieged at Masada in A.D. 72 committed suicide en masse rather than surrender to the Romans. In May 1972, nineteen-year-old Roman Kalanta sat down in a park in Kaunas, the second-largest city in Lithuania, poured a gallon of gasoline over himself, and ignited it. His suicide caused smoldering Lithuanian resistance to Soviet domination to explode into riots, a sitdown strike, and more insistent demands for freedom. But in a great many cases this ultimate, destructive effort to establish control over one's affairs might have been avoided if the person had gained the knowledge and ability to deal with his problems before they became overwhelming.

The number of suicides among young people has increased significantly in the United States. Undoubtedly, this is a result of pressures that begin early in life these days. American society is extremely competitive. That competitiveness has contributed to affluence, world leadership, and such accomplishments as sending men to the moon. It also places such great emphasis on success and achievement that inadequacy at school and parental disapproval have suddenly become insuperable burdens for some students.

Darold Treffert, director of the Winnebago Mental Health Institute in Wisconsin and an authority on suicide, puts part of the blame for the sharp increase in teen-age suicides on what he calls "the American fairy tale." Dr. Treffert says the fairy tale has five themes:

1. More possessions mean more happiness.
2. A person who does, or produces, more is more important.
3. Everyone must belong to and identify with some larger group.
4. Perfect mental health means no problems.
5. A person is abnormal unless constantly happy.

There are other formulas, of course. But a person with suicidal tendencies needs help from a medical or psychiatric counselor. Talking with a parent or teacher could help. But communication is essential.

Some people choose death in more indirect ways. One of the most common forms in our society is reckless driving. Authorities believe that many thousands of unexplained auto deaths are outright or borderline suicides, so close is this behavior pattern to the self-destructive act. Unfortunately, when the automobile is used as the suicide instrument, there can be other innocent victims— passengers, riders in other vehicles, pedestrians. It has been estimated by safety authorities that traffic deaths could be cut by one quarter if everyone wore a seat belt. Using a seat belt is a decision for life. Ignoring the seat belt is a decision for death.

It has also been estimated, by the National Automobile Club, that the drinking of alcohol is involved in half of all traffic deaths. The alcoholic brings about his death in a surer way even if he misses with the automobile. He drinks until his liver gives out. The death certificate lists cirrhosis, one of the fastest growing causes of death in the United States.

Another decision for premature death is the decision to smoke. Smoking is associated with the two main causes of death in the United States—heart disease and cancer. The American Cancer Society estimates that about one American in six dies from causes related to smoking. Regular cigarette smokers are nine times more likely to die from lung cancer than nonsmokers, and the rate is twenty times as high for those who smoke two packs a day or more. A smoker at age twenty-five who smokes a pack or more of cigarettes a day can expect to forefeit six and a half years of his life. That's an average. Some smokers are luckier. Some not so lucky.

Despite the warning by the Surgeon General of the United States that smoking tobacco is a health hazard, the consumption

of cigarettes is climbing . . . with increased use among teen-
agers. The National Clearing House for Smoking and Health estimates that about 15 percent of adolescents twelve to eighteen years
old smoke. According to the Department of Agriculture, about
42 percent of American men and 30 percent of American women
smoke.

This strange custom of a large part of the population indulg-
ing in a life-shortening practice brings us to the industrial ethic,
something else to be acquainted with in order to survive. The
industrial ethic is amoral. That is, it doesn't care what is good or
bad, beneficial or harmful. It is concerned only with what will
make money. Now, a company might refrain from selling a
dangerous product, but it would be mainly motivated by concern
over its own image. A scandal would be bad for business.

As we see, tobacco companies feel no guilt in marketing cigarettes. Nor do their indispensable assistants in the advertising
industry. They sell cigarettes by insinuating that if you smoke
cigarettes you will become attractive like this glamorous movie
star or popular like that well-known entertainer or masculine like
the cowboy or self-confident or adult or whatever the advertisers
think your desire is. If you stop to think about it, many or most
products you see on television are precisely those with the least
worth. They need all the help they can get from commercials.

Your government acts to protect you from cancer-causing
agents. They are banned from the foods you eat and the beverages
you drink. Because of a loophole in our laws, however, the government has not banned cancer-causing agents in what we inhale.
In the case of cigarettes, the Surgeon General's warning is on each
pack, and the Federal Communications Commission has banned
cigarette commercials from television and radio. But you must
also be aware that the federal and state governments collect huge
revenues from taxes on tobacco, so these governments are in no
hurry to ban the sale of cigarettes.

Which brings us back to the industrial ethic. Its motto is: Buyer Beware. Nobody is forcing you to buy a particular product. If you happen to buy cancer and a shorter life, it's your decision. The decision to smoke is a decision for death. The decision not to smoke or to give up smoking is a decision for life.

We have seen a few ways in which behavior influences not only the manner of death but its timing (being overweight is another highway to early death). Now let us turn to feelings, because medical investigators are beginning to determine that our emotions—how we *regard* our circumstances—exert an extremely important influence on our health.

In 1958, Curt Richter, a psychologist at Johns Hopkins Medical School, wrote a paper called "The Phenomenon of Unexplained Sudden Death in Animals and Man." In this report, he explained how he had accidentally become interested in the phenomenon of sudden death.

He had been experimenting with three laboratory rats from which he wanted to get pure urine samples. However, the animals kept dropping bits of food into the funnels that collected their urine. So Dr. Richter decided to cut the rats' whiskers with electric clippers. Afterwards, one of the three rats began acting in a strange fashion. It compulsively buried its head into its food cup with a sort of corkscrewing motion and continued to behave in this manner for as long as the researchers watched—four hours.

When the scientists returned to the laboratory the next morning, the rat was dead. A careful autopsy could reveal no cause or means for the death.

Two years later, Dr. Richter was studying how long rats could swim. Water was kept in motion forcing each rodent to swim continuously. At the optimum temperature of 95 degrees Fahrenheit, the rats could swim on the average for two and a half days. During this experiment Dr. Richter recalled the whisker-trimming incident. He trimmed the whiskers of twelve white rats and put them back in the water-filled jars. One of the rats swam excitedly for a few seconds, dived to the bottom, obviously seeking an escape, then swam below the surface until it suddenly stopped and died.

Autopsy showed no signs of drowning.

One other rat behaved in a similar manner and soon died. The other ten rats went on swimming normally.

At this point, Dr. Richter decided to try his improvised experiment with wild rats, those brown-gray rats you see around exposed garbage cans or at a dump. He repeated the experiment with thirty-four wild rats. Every one of them died within two to eight minutes.

At first, Dr. Richter decided that the loss of its whiskers—one of the rat's chief means of contact with the world—caused sufficient stress to end the creature's life. But when some wild rats died in the same mysterious way even without their whiskers being cut, he realized he was dealing with a more general phenomenon of unexplained sudden death.

He began to think more about the wild Norway rat, the ancestor of the tame laboratory rat. The Norway rat is the most common rat in the world. It differs from the domesticated albino rat in a number of ways. For one thing, its adrenal glands are much larger. The adrenals are those glands that send through our bodies hormones that immediately key us up if we are frightened or angry. They are important defenses for all mammals. They cause generation of sudden energy and prepare the animal for flight or fight. The Norway rat established its supremacy through its fierce, aggressive, suspicious nature. It takes advantage of any possibility to escape, and even after months in the laboratory it is ready to inflict nasty bites.

For this reason, the wild rat requires special handling in order to transport it to the water jars and to cut its whiskers. To remove the rat from its cage, a sliding door is opened to a black bag. See-ing the black hole and thinking it is a way to escape, the rat runs into the bag. By means of a rod, the rat is forced to the bottom of the bag, where a researcher can get a firm grip on its head and body.

Thinking about it afterwards, Dr. Richter was struck by the fact that not a single rat ever attempted to bite through the bag.

Electrodes attached to wild rats in later experiments showed that the heartbeat began to slow almost immediately after it was held tightly inside the black bag. In some cases, the beat speeded up at first, then tapered off until its stopped. The nervous system can cause heartbeat to slow down and even stop as in cases of fright. The expression "He was scared to death" can be literally true.

Dr. Richter believes that when wild rats are held in the black bag, they are confronted by a predicament that cannot be resolved either by fight or flight. They are facing a trial for which neither their evolution nor experience prepared them. They suddenly find themselves utterly helpless. And that appears to trigger an emo-tional response of hopelessness. "Actually," Dr. Richter says, "such a reaction of apparent hopelessness is shown by some wild rats very soon after being grasped in the hand and prevented from moving. They seem literally to give up."

When these rats that have given up are rescued from the wa-ter to discover that their plight is not hopeless, and are then re-turned to the jar, they will begin swimming and continue to do so until their strength gives out, two and a half days later.

Dr. Richter acknowledges that his thinking during these ex-periments was influenced by another scientific paper, written in 1942 by Walter Cannon. Dr. Cannon was an expert in bodily functions who had won great esteem for showing the importance of the autonomic nervous system to our health and welfare. The autonomic nervous system is the one that runs our bodies without our consciously thinking about the process. If we had to remember to tell the heart to beat, and the lungs to breathe, and the palms to sweat, and the body to jump at a sudden noise, we would have no time to think of anything else. We couldn't survive for very long.

Now, while this second nervous system pretty much runs on its own, it is powerfully affected by what we think or feel. If we become frightened, the autonomic system immediately changes the chemical balance in our bodies, getting us prepared to flee if we have to. But the same energy can be turned to fighting our way out of the danger if we decide that is the better course. If we see that we are outnumbered by an enemy and trapped, however, we might elect to give up. We submit to our enemy, although we could still hope for merciful treatment.

The main point is that it is how we perceive a situation—not necessarily the situation itself—that determines our reaction. Usually, our perception coincides with the reality. We usually know when we are in dangerous situations or pleasant ones, and act accordingly. Not always, though, which is why con men so often succeed in stealing money from unsuspecting victims. Sometimes we act inappropriately to the real situation, like the rats that died so quickly in the water jars.

The mystery that Dr. Cannon was interested in was voodoo death—why the victims succumbed to the curse. The key to the mystery, he found, was that they *believed* it.

They believed that their lives were threatened. The belief turned on the fight-or-flight machinery (which Dr. Cannon discovered). But there was no way to fight against the curse, no way to flee from it. No defense. Our bodies were not built to respond to fright (or anger or other intense emotions) indefinitely. When the body is forced by emotions to react at that high level for hours or days without letup, it burns out like a motor that is raced too long.

The voodoo victim realizes that he is helpless. He responds to this realization with a feeling of hopelessness. He gives up, and death is not far behind . . . leaving no cause to satisfy the curiosity of medical examiners.

George Engel, of the University of Rochester Medical School, collected a file of 170 cases of sudden death. He broke down the causes of death into eight categories. Five categories involved helplessness. This lethal combination appeared in a good many of the deaths: highly intense emotion coupled with feelings of helplessness.

If the victim of a hex somehow survives, he can never again be subjected to the voodoo death. He is as immune as anyone else who doesn't believe in it.

Now, what does all this mean to us, to our lives?

Let's put the pieces together. First, we are all born with some bodily weaknesses. They may not be outright defects, but are likely to be spots that are more vulnerable than the rest, the weak links in the chain. When you get sick, it may always be a head cold, but when your sister gets sick, it is a chest cold, while your uncle complains of a bad back, and so on.

Second, stress is an event that puts a strain on us, forces us to mobilize our psychic defenses in order to achieve a readjustment to an altered life situation. The stress can be painful, such as the loss of someone you love or a physical wound. It can be threatening, such as the possible loss of a job. It can even be something good, like winning $100,000 in the lottery. The main thing is that your life circumstances are changed.

Third. We cope with day-to-day stresses without too much trouble and often hardly think of them. As we should. But to major stresses we react with strong emotions necessary to enable our bodies to respond properly. If one or a combination of stresses becomes too severe and lasts too long, the psychological distress we experience initially is translated eventually into sickness, disease, and even death.

Just as certain patterns of behavior can influence the manner of death, so we are predisposed to certain diseases by the weak links in our physical and mental-emotional makeup. How we perceive our life situation and how we react to stress are determined by our feelings, our beliefs, what we have been taught, what we have experienced—the complex array that goes to make up the personality of an individual.

Cancer is a disease that some researchers now see as strongly associated with perceived helplessness and hopelessness . . . and giving up.

Arthur Schmale, Jr., at the University of Rochester Medical School, interviewed fifty-one women who were undergoing examinations to see if they had cancer of the cervix. Previous Pap tests showed that each of the women had some irregular or suspicious but not cancerous cells.

The interviews revealed that eighteen of the women found themselves in some profoundly distressing life situation within six months before the Pap test. These women felt overpowered by feelings of hopelessness. None of the other thirty-three women had such feelings. Dr. Schmale and a co-investigator predicted that the eighteen despairing women would be more likely to have developed cancer while the other thirty-three women would be less likely to have the disease.

The results showed that eleven of the eighteen women who had experienced hopelessness did have cancer; twenty-five or the remaining thirty-three women did not. The predictions were 72 percent accurate.

Lawrence LeShan, a psychotherapist who worked with cancer patients for fifteen years, began to detect a recognizable pattern to the personalities and lives of many cancer victims. The pattern appeared in 72 percent of some 450 patients he interviewed and tested. From early childhood, they had difficulty in establishing loving relationships. They felt rejected, unloved, insecure; and constantly searched for ways to please other people. Afraid of losing whatever regard they enjoyed, they suppressed their own intense feelings of anger, loneliness, despair. Outwardly, though, they appeared to be fine, considerate, gentle people.

Sometime during their adult lives, they enjoyed a period of success that enabled them to experience joy for the first time. They fell in love and married the person they loved. Or suddenly their career took a turn that brought out hidden talents and recognition. Or there were the satisfactions of parenthood.

But this phase came to an end. The beloved husband or wife died, the cherished child left home, the career suffered a reverse. The potential cancer victim reverted to the earlier pattern. He felt isolated but never expressed the rage and other intense emotions he felt inwardly. And he did not ask "Why me?" He seemed to accept his fate as if he had always known it was going to happen. Despite the inner torment, he appeared to others to be a calm person, brave and cheerful. Within six months to eight years, cancer appeared.

If many cancer victims are passive and accepting of their fate, candidates for heart attacks are just the opposite. They often have aggressive personalities, often have difficulty in concealing their hostility to authority, and cannot easily take discipline. "Most cardiac patients that I have seen," says Dr. Hutschnecker, "have struck me as reckless gamblers with life; when they reach an impasse, they think in terms of dying rather than accepting humiliation or defeat."

Again, as many investigators now strongly suspect, it is the personality with a characteristic pattern of emotional responses that sets up the disease. What we are seeing in our present-day civilization are countless threats and challenges that evolution never prepared our bodies to cope with. Office competition for advancement or irritation between a boss and worker are typical triggers of the fight-or-flight response. The hypothalamus in the brain signals the adrenal glands to send their hormones through the body. The body begins using more oxygen, breathing is deeper, the heart beats faster, pumping more blood, and more blood is sent to the muscles.

But there is no action, no resolution. The person can neither fight physically nor run away. Popping the boss on the nose or quitting means loss of the job.

It is now beginning to appear that continual stimulation of this fight-or-flight response without taking any action is one of the most harmful things that can happen to us. Adrenaline breaks down stored fat so that fatty acids can flow through the blood-stream to supply more energy as it is needed by the muscles for the anticipated crisis. If the fatty acids are not used, they can be restored or used to make cholesterol. A continuous high level of fats in the blood increases the likelihood that a fatty surface will build up along the inner walls of blood vessels, narrowing the passageway and setting the stage for a heart attack.

Also, each time the response is set off, blood vessels are pinched in order to heighten blood pressure so that blood can be forced into the muscles. But if this system is in a continual state of ex-citation, the blood vessels do not relax. High blood pressure, or hypertension as it is known medically, is a notorious precursor of strokes and heart attacks.

Smoking, far from relaxing a person, stimulates the heart and tightens blood vessels, compounding the situation. Obviously, exercise would burn off the fat energy mobilized in the blood-stream and provide an outlet for the physical action for which the body has prepared itself. Exercise also keeps the body trim, and being overweight is a visible precondition for heart disease. Each extra pound of fatty tissue requires an additional mile of capil-laries to nourish it, putting that much more strain on the heart.

But, alas, most pursuits in our highly technological civilization are sedentary. They make substantial psychological, emotional, and mental demands and impose physical ease. The results of the latest research, writes physician Malcolm Carruthers in *The Western Way of Death,* "suggest that in modern society wrath, reinforced by sloth and gluttony, is the deadliest of the seven sins."

For the first time in history, really, we are realizing just how much influence a young person can exert over his life, shortening it or lengthening it. He can establish those attitudes and habits, on the basis of what science is revealing, that will promote a more satisfying life, and a longer one.

Back in 1955, the National Institute of Mental Health began a long-term study of elderly men. At that time, their average age was seventy-one years. All forty-seven of the subjects were essentially in good health. The study examined more than six hundred characteristics of the men's physical condition and behavior. Twelve years later, twenty-four of the men were dead, twenty-three of them still alive. The investigators set down the characteristics they considered the most important in surviving. Survivors did better in intelligence tests, were more involved in social relationships, could handle loss better, had high self-esteem, and were better in running their day-to-day lives.

What is most interesting is that of all the characteristics studied, two main ones were more significant in separating the quick from the dead. The men who survived were better at organizing their daily lives and they did not smoke.

Duke University conducted a somewhat similar study, except that it covered 256 people—women as well as men, unhealthy as well as healthy—who were sixty years and older. The study found four ways to predict which people would live the longest. In order of importance, these predictors are:

1. Getting satisfaction from work, a person's feeling of general usefulness in society
2. Happiness, a person's general satisfaction with his life situation

Bibliography

In writing *Living with Death*, I found especially useful a pioneering work on the subject, *The Meaning of Death* edited by Herman Feifel and published in 1959, particularly "Personality Factors in Dying Patients" by Arnold A. Hutschnecker and "The Phenomenon of Unexplained Sudden Death in Animals and Man" by Curt P. Richter, among other excellent articles. I also recommend *Death and Dying* edited by Leonard Pearson, *Concerning Death: A Practical Guide for the Living* by Earl A. Grollman (which is fine for anyone wanting a single handbook on the subject), *Loss and Grief* by Bernard Schoenberg et al., *Death As a Fact of Life* by David Hendin, *Western Attitudes Toward Death* by Philippe Ariès, *The Western Way of Death* by Malcolm Carruthers, *Man Against Himself* by Karl Menninger; the classics, *The Golden Bough* by Sir James Frazer and *Magic, Science and Religion* by Bronislaw Malinowski; and an article by Maggie Scarf, "The Anatomy of Fear."

Alvarez, A. *The Savage God*. New York: Random, 1972 (Bantam paperback).

Ariès, Philippe. *Western Attitudes Toward Death*. Baltimore: Johns Hopkins, 1974.

Arlen, Michael J. "The Cold, Bright Charms of Immortality" in *The New Yorker* (January 27, 1975).

Barden, J. C. "Calvary Gives Terminal Patients an 'Integrated' Approach to Death" in *The New York Times* (May 3, 1973).

Benson, Herbert. "Your Innate Asset for Combating Stress" in *Harvard Business Review* (July–August 1974)

Brim, Orville G., Jr., et al. *The Dying Patient*. New York: Russell Sage Foundation, 1970.

Cadwalader, Mary H. "Early Warnings of Future Disaster" in *Smithsonian* (May 1974).

Cannon, Walter B. " 'Voodoo' Death" in *American Anthropologist* (April–June 1942).

Carruthers, Malcolm. *The Western Way of Death*. New York: Pantheon, 1974.

Choron, Jacques. *Death and Modern Man*. New York: Macmillan, 1964.

Cutler, Donald R. *Updating Life and Death*. Boston: Beacon, 1968.

Dempsey, David. "The Living Will—and the Will to Live" in *The New York Times Magazine* (June 23, 1974).

Durant, Will. *The Story of Philosophy*. New York: Simon & Schuster, 1926.

Emerson, Ralph Waldo. "Compensation" from the *Complete Essays and Other Writings of Ralph Waldo Emerson*. New York: Random, 1940, 1950.

Erikson, Erik H. *Childhood and Society*. New York: Norton, 1950.

Esfandiary, F. M. "Sorry, We're Here for Eternity" in *The New York Times* (September 25, 1974).

Ettinger, Robert C. W. *The Prospect of Immortality*. Garden City: Doubleday, 1964 (Macfadden-Bartell paperback).

Evans, W. E. D. *The Chemistry of Death*. Springfield, Ill.: Thomas, 1963.

Faulkner, William. "A Rose for Emily" from *The Faulkner Reader*. New York: Random, 1930.

Feifel, Herman. *The Meaning of Death*. New York: McGraw-Hill, 1959.

Frankfort, Henri et al. *Before Philosophy*. Baltimore: Penguin, 1949.

Frazer, James G. *The Golden Bough*. New York: Macmillan, 1922, 1947.

Glaser, Barney G., and Strauss, Anselm L. *Awareness of Dying*. Chicago: Aldine, 1965.

Gordon, David Cole. *Overcoming the Fear of Death*. New York: Macmillan, 1970.

Grollman, Earl A. *Concerning Death: A Practical Guide for the Living*. Boston: Beacon, 1974.

———. *Explaining Death to Children*. Boston: Beacon, 1967.

Harrington, Alan. *The Immortalist.* New York: Random, 1969.

Hendin, David. *Death As a Fact of Life.* New York: Norton, 1973 (Warner paperback).

Hinton, John. *Dying.* Baltimore: Penguin, 1967, 1972.

Huxley, Aldous. *Ends and Means.* New York: Harper, 1937.

Kübler-Ross, Elisabeth. *On Death and Dying.* New York: Macmillan, 1969.

———. *Questions and Answers on Death and Dying.* New York: Macmillan, 1974.

———. "Let's Only Talk About the Present" in *The New York Times* (January 15, 1973). Excerpts from testimony by Dr. Ross before the Senate Special Committee on Aging.

Lifton, Robert Jay, and Olson, Eric. *Living and Dying.* New York: Praeger, 1974.

Malinowski, Bronislaw. *Magic, Science and Religion.* Garden City: Doubleday, 1948, 1954.

Mannes, Marya. *Last Rights.* New York: Morrow, 1973 (New American Library paperback).

Marris, Peter. "The Meaning of Grief" in *The New York Times* (March 10, 1975).

Menninger, Karl A. *Man Against Himself.* New York: Harcourt, Brace, 1938.

Mitford, Jessica. *The American Way of Death.* New York: Simon & Schuster, 1963 (Fawcett paperback).

Murphy, Gardner. *Three Papers on the Survival Problem.* New York: American Society for Psychical Research, 1945.

Pasternak, Boris. *Doctor Zhivago.* New York: Pantheon, 1958.

Pearson, Leonard. *Death and Dying.* Cleveland: Case Western Reserve, 1969.

Rubin, Theodore Isaac. *The Winner's Notebook.* New York: Trident, 1967.

Scarf, Maggie. "The Anatomy of Fear" in *The New York Times Magazine* (June 16, 1974).

Schoenberg, Bernard, et al. *Loss and Grief.* New York: Columbia, 1970.

Segerberg, Osborn, Jr. *The Immortality Factor.* New York: Dutton, 1974.

Shneidman, Edwin. "You & Death" in *Psychology Today* (June 1971).

Simpson, George Gaylord. *The Meaning of Evolution*. New Haven: Yale, 1949, 1967 (Bantam paperback).

Slagle, Alton. "A Doctor Looks Beyond Death" in *New York Sunday News* (August 4, 1974).

Stevenson, Ian. *Twenty Cases Suggestive of Reincarnation*. New York: American Society for Psychical Research, 1966.

Thomas, Lewis. *The Lives of a Cell*. New York: Viking, 1974.

Toynbee, Arnold, et al. *Man's Concern with Death*. New York: McGraw-Hill, 1968.

Waugh, Evelyn. *The Loved One*. Boston: Little, Brown, 1948 (Dell paperback).

Wilder, Thornton. *Our Town*. New York: Harper & Row, 1938, 1957.

Winter, Arthur. *The Moment of Death*. Springfield, Ill.: Thomas, 1969.

Wyschogrod, Edith. *The Phenomenon of Death*. New York: Harper & Row, 1973.

Index

128
S   Segerberg, Osborn
            Living with death

26941-HC

DATE			
MAR 2 5 1980	MAY 2 6 1981	FEB 2 8 1985	JAN 0 7
APR 8 1980	OCT 2 1 1982	MAY 18	FEB 2 0
APR 1 5 1980		MAY 2 5	MAR 3 1
APR 2 2 1980	FEB 18 1981	JUN 9	
APR 2 9 1980	OCT 2 6 1982	SEP 21	MAY 0 5
MAY 6 1980	EB 1 5 1982	SEP 21	
OCT 2 1980	MAR 1 5 1983	NOV 23	
	NOV 1 5	JAN 0 0 1991	
OCT 9 1980	DEC 1 3	JAN 23 1991	
OCT 3 0 1980	APR 19	SEP 1 0	
MAY 1 9 1981	JAN 1 5 1984	OCT 1 5 1991	
	FEB 2 1		

© THE BAKER & TAYLOR CO.